SRA OPEN COURT READING

SRA

A Division of The McGraw-Hill Companies

Columbus, Ohio

www.sra4kids.com

SRA/McGraw-Hill

A Division of The McGraw·Hill Companies

Send all inquiries to:
SRA/McGraw-Hill
8787 Orion Place
Columbus, OH 43240-4027

Printed in the United States of America.

ISBN 0-07-572028-0

2 3 4 5 6 7 8 9 POH 07 06 05 04 03 02

Table of Contents

Unit 1   Sharing Stories

Lesson 1   *Ant and the Three Little Figs*
Spelling: The *gl*, *bl*, and *pl* Blends. 2
Vocabulary: Vocabulary Strategies. 3
Grammar and Usage:
Common and Proper Nouns 4

Lesson 2   *Come Back, Jack!*
Comprehension: Compare and Contrast. . . . 5
Spelling: The *gr*, *dr*, and *tr* Blends 7
Vocabulary: Context Clues. 8
Writer's Craft: Time and Order Words. 9
Grammar and Usage:
Subject and Object Pronouns 10

Lesson 3   *The Library*
Spelling: The Final /k/ Sound 11
Vocabulary: Word Structure. 12

Grammar and Usage: Action Verbs. 13
Writer's Craft: Beginnings and Endings . . . 14

Lesson 4   *Story Hour—Starring Megan!*
Comprehension: Making Inferences 15
Spelling: The *nd* and *st* Blends 17
Vocabulary: Dictionary. 18
Grammar and Usage:
Possessive Nouns and Pronouns 19
Writer's Craft: Staying on the Topic 20

Lesson 5   *Tomás and the Library Lady*
Comprehension: Point of View 21
Spelling: Review. 23
Vocabulary: Thesaurus. 24
Grammar and Usage: Review 25

Unit 2   Kindness

Lesson 1   *Mushroom in the Rain*
Comprehension: Drawing Conclusions. . . . 26
Spelling: The /a/ Sound 28
Vocabulary: Base Word Families 29
Mechanics: Capitalization at the
Beginning of Sentences 30
Writer's Craft: Tone of a Personal Letter . . 31

Lesson 2   *The Elves and the Shoemaker*
Comprehension: Sequence. 32
Spelling: The /e/ Sound 34
Vocabulary: Homophones 35
Mechanics: Commas in
Greetings and Closings 36
Writer's Craft: Sentence Elaboration. 37

Lesson 3   *The Paper Crane*
Spelling: The /i/ Sound. 38
Vocabulary: Levels of
Specificity Categories 39
Mechanics: Capitalization of
Months and Days 40
Writer's Craft: Personal Letter Structure . . 41

Lesson 4   *Butterfly House*
Spelling: The /o/ and /aw/ Sounds. 42

Vocabulary: Multiple Meanings 43
Mechanics: Commas in a Series 44
Writer's Craft: Time and Order Words. 45

Lesson 5   *Corduroy*
Comprehension: Making Inferences 46
Spelling: The /u/ Sound 48
Vocabulary: Homographs 49
Mechanics: Quotation Marks
and Underlining 50
Writer's Craft: Sensory Details. 51

Lesson 6   *The Story of Three Whales*
Spelling: The Final /ən/ Sound 52
Vocabulary: Shades of Meaning. 53
Mechanics: Commas in
City, State, Dates 54
Writer's Craft: Structure of a
Business Letter 55

Lesson 7   *Cinderella*
Spelling: Review. 56
Vocabulary: Review 57
Grammar, Usage, and Mechanics:
Review 58
Writer's Craft: Background Information . . . 59

Unit 3 Look Again

Lesson 1 *I See Animals Hiding*
Spelling: The /ā/ Sound 60
Vocabulary: Base Word Families 61
Grammar and Usage:
Sentences and End Marks 62
Writer's Craft: Expository Structure 63
Writer's Craft: Topic Sentences 64

Lesson 2 *They Thought They Saw Him*
Comprehension: Drawing Conclusions 65
Spelling: The /ē/ Sound 67
Vocabulary: Prefixes 68
Grammar and Usage:
Linking and Helping Verbs 69
Writer's Craft: Note Taking 70

Lesson 3 *Hungry Little Hare*
Spelling: The /ī/ Sound 71
Vocabulary: Compound Words 72
Grammar and Usage:
Subject/Verb Agreement 73
Writer's Craft: Transition Words 74

Lesson 4 *How to Hide an Octopus and
Other Sea Creatures*
Spelling: The /ō/ Sound 75

Vocabulary: Suffixes 76
Grammar and Usage:
Parts of a Sentence 77
Writer's Craft: Expository Structure 78
Writer's Craft: Supporting Details 79

Lesson 5 *How the Guinea Fowl Got
Her Spots*
Comprehension:
Classify and Categorize 80
Spelling: The /o͞o/ Sound 82
Vocabulary: Suffixes 83
Grammar and Usage:
Complete Sentences 84
Writer's Craft:
Place and Location Words 85

Lesson 6 *Animal Camouflage*
Comprehension: Main Idea 86
Spelling: Review 88
Vocabulary: Suffixes 89
Grammar and Usage: Review 90
Writer's Craft: Fact and Opinion 91

Unit 4 Fossils

Lesson 1 *Fossils Tell of Long Ago*
Spelling: Words with *wh* and *sh* 92
Vocabulary: Concept Words 93
Grammar and Usage: Adjectives 94

Lesson 2 *The Dinosaur Who Lived
in My Backyard*
Comprehension: Fact and Opinion 95
Spelling: Words with *ch* and *th* 97
Vocabulary: Synonyms 98
Grammar and Usage: Contractions 99
Writer's Craft: Rhyme 100

Lesson 3 *Dinosaur Fossils*
Comprehension: Classify and Categorize . 101
Spelling: The /ar/ Sound 103
Vocabulary: Science Words 104
Grammar and Usage: Verb Tenses 105
Writer's Craft: Figurative Language 106

Lesson 4 *Why Did the Dinosaurs
Disappear?*
Spelling: The /er/ and /or/ Sounds 107

Vocabulary: Antonyms 108
Grammar and Usage:
Nouns: Singular and Plural 109
Writer's Craft:
Descriptive Organization 110
Writer's Craft:
Collecting and Organizing Data 111

Lesson 5 *Monster Tracks*
Comprehension: Sequence 112
Spelling: Words with *br* and *fr* 114
Vocabulary: Analogies 115
Grammar and Usage: Adverbs 116
Writer's Craft:
Paragraph Form 117

Lesson 6 *Let's Go Dinosaur Tracking!*
Spelling: Review 118
Vocabulary: Review 119
Grammar and Usage: Review 120
Writer's Craft: Topic Sentences 121

Unit 5 Courage

Lesson 1 *Molly the Brave and Me*
Comprehension: Point of View 122
Spelling: Words Ending in *-ed* and *-ing* . . . 124
Vocabulary: Synonyms 125
Mechanics: Capitalization of
Proper Nouns 126
Writer's Craft: Narrative Organization . . . 127

Lesson 2 *Dragons and Giants*
Spelling: Present Tense of Words 128
Vocabulary: Antonyms 129
Grammar and Usage:
Conjunctions and Interjections 130
Writer's Craft: Plot 131
Writer's Craft: Suspense and Surprise 132

Lesson 3 *The Hole in the Dike*
Comprehension: Cause and Effect 133
Spelling: Past Tense of Words 135
Vocabulary: Base Word Families 136
Mechanics: Commas in Dialogue 137
Writer's Craft: Characterization 138
Writer's Craft: Setting 139

Lesson 4 *A Picture Book of
Martin Luther King, Jr.*
Spelling: Plurals 140
Vocabulary: Prefixes 141
Mechanics: Capitalization of
Titles and Initials 142
Writer's Craft: Dialogue 143

Lesson 5 *The Empty Pot*
Comprehension: Sequence 144
Spelling: Suffixes 146
Vocabulary: Suffixes 147
Mechanics: Apostrophes and Colons 148
Writer's Craft: Sentence Combining 149

Lesson 6 *Brave as a Mountain Lion*
Comprehension: Author's Purpose 150
Spelling: Review 152
Vocabulary: Prefixes 153
Grammar, Usage, and Mechanics:
Review 154
Writer's Craft: Time and Order Words 155

Unit 6 Our Country and Its People

Lesson 1 *The First Americans*
Spelling: Prefixes 156
Vocabulary: Social Studies Words 157
Grammar, Usage, and Mechanics:
Review 158
Writer's Craft: Audience and Purpose 159

Lesson 2 *New Hope*
Comprehension: Cause and Effect 160
Spelling: Suffixes 162
Vocabulary: Suffixes 163
Grammar, Usage, and Mechanics:
Review 164
Writer's Craft: Words of Request 165

Lesson 3 *A Place Called Freedom*
Spelling: Compound Words 166
Vocabulary: Compound Words 167
Grammar, Usage, and Mechanics:
Review 168
Writer's Craft: Structure of Scripts 169

Lesson 4 *The Story of the Statue of Liberty*
Spelling: Homophones 170
Vocabulary: Homophones 171

Grammar, Usage, and Mechanics:
Adjectives, Adverbs, and Contractions . . . 172

Lesson 5 *The Butterfly Seeds*
Comprehension: Making Inferences 173
Spelling: Homographs 175
Vocabulary: Homographs 176
Grammar, Usage, and Mechanics:
Review 177
Writer's Craft: Words of Request 178

Lesson 6 *A Piece of Home*
Spelling: Words with Foreign Origins 179
Vocabulary: Multicultural Words 180
Grammar, Usage, and Mechanics:
Review 181
Writer's Craft: Supporting Details 182

Lesson 7 *Jalapeño Bagels*
Comprehension: Fact and Opinion 183
Spelling: Review 185
Vocabulary: Review 186
Grammar, Usage, and Mechanics:
Review 187
Writer's Craft: Plagiarism 188

UNIT I **Sharing Stories • Lesson I** *Ant and the Three Little Figs*

▶The *gl*, *bl*, and *pl* Blends

SPELLING

Say the word *play*. The letters *p* and *l* make their own sounds, but are said so quickly that the sounds blend together. The blends *gl*, *bl*, and *pl* are often heard at the beginning of words.

Practice

block	plus	blink	glue	blend

 Vowel-Substitution Strategy Replace the underlined vowel or vowels with the new letter. The blend will be spelled the same.

1. gl<u>ee</u> + u = **glue** _____

2. bl<u>a</u>nk + i = **blink** _____

3. pl<u>ow</u>s + u = **plus** _____

4. bl<u>a</u>ck + o = **block** _____

5. bl<u>i</u>nd + e = **blend** _____

The gl, bl, and pl Blends • **Reteach**

▶Vocabulary Strategies

> The sentence you are reading may give you clues to what a word might mean.

Practice **Fill in the blank with a word from the box. The underlined words will help you decide which word to use. After you finish the sentence, read it aloud. Does it sound like you chose the right word?**

carrots	horse	airplane	raisins	fly

1. He swatted at the _____ fly _____, but the tiny <u>insect</u> with <u>wings</u> came right back.

2. I put a <u>saddle</u> on the _____ horse _____, and made sure his <u>tail</u> was brushed.

3. She loves to <u>fly</u> in an _____ airplane _____, because <u>riding</u> so <u>high</u> in the <u>air</u> is fun.

4. The horse <u>ate</u> the <u>orange</u> _____ carrots _____, his favorite <u>snack</u>.

5. I love <u>fruit</u>, especially <u>tiny</u> _____ raisins _____, which are yummy in cookies.

VOCABULARY

▶ Common and Proper Nouns

GRAMMAR AND USAGE

> **Common nouns** *do not* begin with a capital letter.
> **Proper nouns** *do* begin with a capital letter.
>
> | **Rule** | **Example** |
> |---|---|
> | ▶ A common noun is a person, place, or thing. | ▶ city, team, state, dog |
> | ▶ A proper noun *names* a person, place, or thing. | ▶ Los Angeles, San Diego, California, Spot |

Practice

▶ Write *common* or *proper* on the line for each noun.

1. elephant   **common** _____

2. Wyoming   **proper** _____

3. Stephen   **proper** _____

▶ **Underline the proper nouns in each sentence. Circle the common nouns.**

4. <u>Juanita</u> went to <u>Dallas</u> on her (vacation.)

5. <u>Dallas</u> is a (city) in <u>Texas</u>.

6. The (state) of <u>Texas</u> borders the (country) of <u>Mexico</u>.

▶ Compare and Contrast

Focus Writers sometimes compare and contrast in a story to make an idea clearer and to make the story more interesting.

▶ To **compare** means to tell how two or more things are **alike**. Clue words *like*, *same*, *as*, *both*, *also*, and *too* are used.

   Cheetahs and tigers are *both* cats.

▶ To **contrast** means to tell how two or more things are **different**. Clue words *different* and *but* are used.

   Tigers have stripes, *but* cheetahs have spots.

Practice Look at the two things listed. Explain how the two are alike and how they are different.

1. bird's nest   house

   Answers will vary. Possible answers are shown.

How are they alike? **They are both homes.** _____

_____

How are they different? **Materials they are made of;** _____

who lives there; where they are. _____

COMPREHENSION

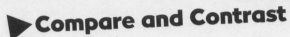

Compare and Contrast

COMPREHENSION

2. bicycle   car

How are they alike? **They are both used for**

transportation.

How are they different? **A car has an engine. A bicycle**

has pedals.

3. sheep   cow

How are they alike? **They are both farm animals.**

How are they different? **A sheep is valued for its fleece.**

A cow gives milk we drink. They make different noises.

 Write the name of your favorite television
show and your favorite book. Then tell how
they are alike and different.

Television show: **Answers will vary.**

Book: _____

How are they alike? _____

How are they different? _____

Name _____ Date _____

▶The *gr*, *dr*, and *tr* Blends

Say the word *tray*. The letters *t* and *r* make their own sounds, but are said so quickly that the sounds blend together. The blends *gr*, *dr*, and *tr* are often heard at the beginning of words.

Practice

tree	drum	gray	truck	drip

 Meaning Strategy Write the word from the box that best fits in the sentence.

1. Black and white blend to make _____ **gray** _____.

2. The leaf fell from the _____ **tree** _____.

3. A _____ **drip** _____ fell from the icicle.

4. The band member beat the _____ **drum** _____.

5. A worker drove the big _____ **truck** _____.

SPELLING

▶ Context Clues

VOCABULARY

> *Context clues* are words that help you figure out what a hard word might mean.
> **This waiter serves food and drinks.**
> **Hard word:** waiter
> **Context clues:** serves, food, drinks

Practice   **Read each sentence. Use the underlined clues to help you figure out and write what the hard word means.**

Answers will vary

1. The <u>small</u>, <u>wild</u> lynx looked like a <u>cat</u> <u>with</u> <u>spots</u>.

   lynx means: **small wildcat with spots** _____

2. The <u>soaking</u> <u>wet</u> children were drenched by the rainstorm.

   drenched means: **soaking wet** _____

3. I <u>partly</u> <u>closed</u> my <u>eyes</u>; my friend also squinted.

   squinted means: **partly closed eyes** _____

4. The leaves quivered and <u>shook</u> <u>slightly</u> in the breeze.

   quivered means: **shook slightly** _____

Name _____ Date _____

▶ Time and Order Words

> Some words tell when something happens. Other words
> tell the order that things happen.
>
> Here are some examples of time and order words.
>
> | Time Words | Order Words |
> |---|---|
> | today | first |
> | yesterday | then |
> | tomorrow | finally |

Practice   Read each sentence. Underline the time
and order words. Then write *time* if it is
a time word or *order* if it is an order
word.

1. <u>Yesterday</u> I rode my bike. _____ **time** _____

2. <u>First</u>, I put on shorts and a T-shirt. _____ **order** _____

3. <u>Then</u>, I put on my helmet. _____ **order** _____

4. <u>Finally</u>, I got on my bike. _____ **order** _____

5. I rode to the school, <u>then</u> to the park. _____ **order** _____

6. <u>Tomorrow</u>, I will go for another ride. _____ **time** _____

WRITER'S CRAFT

▶ Subject and Object Pronouns

GRAMMAR AND USAGE

Rule	**Example**
▶ **Subject pronouns** replace the subjects in sentences.	▶ **Steven** threw the ball to me. **He** threw the ball to me.
▶ Subject pronouns: I, you, he, she, it, we, and they.	
▶ **Object pronouns** replace the objects in sentences.	▶ Steven threw the ball to **Katie**. He threw the ball to **her**.
▶ Object pronouns: me, you, him, her, it, us, and them.	

Practice

▶ **Underline the subject pronoun in each sentence.**

1. I am learning to play the violin.

2. He played the piano.

3. She enjoys music.

▶ **Underline the object pronoun in each sentence.**

4. My father gave me Beethoven's music on CD.

5. My mother plays the piano for us.

UNIT I   Sharing Stories • **Lesson 3** *The Library*

▶The Final /k/ Sound

> The letters *k* and *ck* often spell the /k/ sound at the end of words.
>
> shar<u>k</u>   lo<u>ck</u>

Practice

park	kick	book	stick	dark

 Rhyming Strategy

▶Write the words from the box that rhyme with *mark*.

1. dark _____

2. park _____

▶Write the words from the box that rhyme with *sick*.

3. kick _____

4. stick _____

▶Write the word from the box that rhymes with *look*.

5. book _____

SPELLING

▶ Word Structure

Looking at *word structure*, or different parts inside a word, may help you figure out what a hard word might mean.

I turned the doorknob to open the door.
hard word: doorknob
clues: door, knob

VOCABULARY

Practice **Read each sentence. Look for words inside the underlined word. Figure out what the hard word means and fill in the blanks.**

1. My dogs love to sleep in the sunlight.

   sunlight means: _____**light**_____ from the _____**sun**_____

2. They also like to sleep by the fireplace.

   fireplace means: a _____**place**_____ for a _____**fire**_____

3. Sometimes, they even sleep in my bedroom.

   bedroom means: a _____**room**_____ with a _____**bed**_____

4. They never sleep in the doghouse.

   doghouse means: a _____**house**_____ for a _____**dog**_____

▶Action Verbs

Rule	Example
▶An **action verb** tells what someone or something is doing. It is the word in a sentence that tells what is happening.	▶Noah **rides** a bike. We **walked** on the trails. Sheila **ran** through the field. Thomas **picked** flowers.

Practice

▶Circle the action verbs in the following list of words.

car   (drove)   (throw)

baseball   (hit)   lamp

(shines)   bicycle   (cleaned)

▶Underline the action verb in each sentence.

1. The pilgrims <u>sailed</u> across the ocean.

2. They <u>planted</u> corn in the fields.

3. The Native Americans <u>helped</u> them grow food.

4. They <u>built</u> a village.

5. They <u>fished</u> in the ocean and in lakes.

GRAMMAR AND USAGE

Name _____ Date _____

▶ Beginnings and Endings

A good beginning gets readers to read the rest of the story.
All writing should have a good ending.

WRITER'S CRAFT

Practice   **This paragraph needs improvement. Write a better beginning and ending on the lines.**

Purple Monster was chasing Little Rabbit.

Little Rabbit ran faster and faster, but Purple

Monster was getting closer. Then along

came Mr. Bear on his motorcycle. The end.

Answers will vary.

_____

_____

_____

_____

_____

_____

_____

_____

▶ Making Inferences

Focus   Sometimes a writer does not tell the reader everything. Readers must use what they already know to understand the story.

> Readers can use what they already know to figure out details the author left out.
>
> Here is an example.
> > *John wore his raincoat to school.*
>
> I know that I wear my raincoat when it rains, so it must have been raining when John went to school.

Practice   Read each sentence below. Look for clues in the sentences that can help you figure out more information. Then, circle the statement that best fits the clues in the sentence.

1. Ted shouted, "Come on, Lucky, fetch the stick!"

(Lucky is Ted's pet dog.)

Lucky is Ted's older brother.

2. The only light came from a far-off campfire and the moon shining between the branches.

It is almost morning.

(It is nighttime in a forest.)

COMPREHENSION

▶ **Making Inferences**

COMPREHENSION

3. We clapped and cheered until they raised the curtain for another bow.

(An audience enjoyed a performance.)

It was a very long performance.

Apply **Read the paragraph below. Then, answer the questions.** **Answers will vary.**

School will be starting in two weeks. Marisa has met her new teacher and has seen her classroom. Her mom bought her school supplies a month ago. Her outfit for the first day of school is already picked out.

How does Marisa feel about school starting?

Marisa seems anxious; she could be excited.

_____

What clues tell you that?

She has already seen her classroom and met her teacher.

She has bought her supplies and has picked out her outfit.

_____

_____

▶The *nd* and *st* Blends

> Say the word *stand*. The letters *n* and *d* make their own sounds, but are said so quickly that the sounds blend together.
>
> Remember, the blend *nd* is never found at the beginning of words.

SPELLING

Practice

lost	just	fast	land	stuck

 Vowel-Substitution Strategy Replace the underlined vowel or vowels with the new letter. The blend will be spelled the same. Underline the *nd* or *st* blend in the new word.

1. li̲st + o = <u>lo<u>st</u></u>

2. st<u>a</u>ck + u = <u>st̲u̲c̲k̲</u>

3. l<u>e</u>nd + a = <u>la<u>nd</u></u>

4. f<u>i</u>st + a = <u>fa<u>st</u></u>

5. j<u>o</u>ust + u = <u>ju<u>st</u></u>

▶ Dictionary

A dictionary is a book that shows what words mean.

bird/brown

bird /burd/ *n.* an animal that has wings, two legs, and a body covered with feathers.
birthday /burth′dā/ *n.* **1.** the day on which a person is born. **2.** the return each year of this day.
bite /bīt/ *v.* **bit, bit ten,** or **bit, bit ing. 1.** to seize, cut into, or pierce with the teeth. **2.** to wound with teeth, fangs, or a stinger. *-n.* **1.** a

bottle /bot′əl/ n. a container, usually made of glass or plastic, which holds liquids.
–v. **bot tled bot tling.** to put in bottles.
boy /boi/ n. a very young male child.
brainstorm /brān′ storm/ *n.* a sudden, bright idea; inspiration.

Practice

1. The **entry word** in a dictionary is the word you look up. These words are in ABC order. **Does the word *bird* or *boy* come first in a dictionary?** <u>bird</u>

2. At the top of each dictionary page are two words called **guide words.** These words are the first and last words on a dictionary page. **If we could see the whole page, what would the last word on the page be?** <u>brown</u>

3. A **definition** is the meaning of a word. **Fill in the blanks to complete the definition of *bite*.** Bite: to seize, <u>cut into</u>, or pierce <u>with the teeth</u>.

▶Possessive Nouns and Possessive Pronouns

A **possessive noun** shows ownership.

Rule	**Example**
▶Add an **apostrophe s** (**'s**) to most singular nouns.	▶Jessica**'s** bicycle is red.
▶Add an **apostrophe** (**'**) to plural nouns that end in *s*.	▶The cats**'** toys were on the floor.
▶A **possessive pronoun** can be used instead of a possessive noun.	▶Luke**'s** dad is a firefighter. **His** dad is a firefighter.

Possessive pronouns: *my, your, his, her, its, their,* and *our*.

⟨Practice⟩

Rewrite each phrase using a possessive noun.

1. the book that belongs to Alice _____ Alice's book _____

2. the car of my parents _____ my parents' car _____

Fill in the blank with a possessive pronoun.

Answers may vary.

3. _____ car is red.

▶ Staying on Topic

WRITER'S CRAFT

> Staying on the topic is very important. If you stray from the topic, readers will be confused.
>
> Make a plan before you write. Put your ideas in a graphic organizer.
>
> Ask questions to help you stay on the topic.
>
> ▶ Did I tell my topic in the first few sentences?
>
> ▶ Do I have any details that don't belong?
>
> ▶ Do all my sentences stay on the topic?

Practice **Read the sentences below. Cross out sentences that do not stay on the topic.**

Topic: Florida is a nice place to visit.

1. Florida has nice weather.

2. Florida is near the ocean.

3. ~~My mom grew up in Florida.~~

4. There is a lot to do in Florida.

5. ~~Georgia is near Florida.~~

▶ Point of View

Focus Point of view is how the author decides to tell the story—through a character or through someone outside of the story.

When a story is told from the **first-person point of view**,

▶ the storyteller is a character in the story.

▶ the clue words *I*, *me*, *my*, *us*, and *we* are used.
  I ran to the barn to check the cows.

When a story is told from the **third-person point of view**,

▶ the storyteller is not a character in the story.

▶ the clue words *she*, *her*, *he*, *him*, *they* and *them* are used.
  He looked at the big library.

Practice Read each sentence. Fill in the circle to tell if the sentence is written from the first-person point of view or the third-person point of view. Underline the word or words in each sentence that help you know the point of view.

1. Early one morning, a giant bug crawled up <u>my</u> wall.

   ● first-person point of view

   ○ third-person point of view

COMPREHENSION

▶ **Point of View**

2. <u>She</u> looked at <u>her</u> long hair in the mirror.

    ○ first-person point of view

    ● third-person point of view

3. Tim and <u>I</u> held a jumping contest.

    ● first-person point of view

    ○ third-person point of view

Apply **Read the paragraph below. Circle each word that gives a clue about who is telling the story. Write the point of view on the line.**

(I) was standing at the bus stop with (my) mother. She was holding (my) hand. (We) were looking down the street to see if the bus was coming. (I) could not see it yet. (My) mother knew (I) was feeling nervous. She kissed (me.) It was (my) first day at the new school.

Point of view: **first-person point of view**

COMPREHENSION

▶ Review

The letters *b* and *l* are said quickly together at the beginning of a word. The /k/ sound is spelled *k* or *ck* at the end of a word.

Practice

blind	trick	blue	walk	sock

 Visualization Strategy Circle the correctly spelled word. Then write the word.

1. plue   (blue)   **blue** _____

2. (sock)   sok   **sock** _____

3. walck   (walk)   **walk** _____

4. blid   (blind)   **blind** _____

5. (trick)   trik   **trick** _____

SPELLING

▶ Thesaurus

VOCABULARY

> A **thesaurus** is a book with lists of words with similar meanings. These words are called **synonyms.** Words in a thesaurus are in ABC order.
> Smile is a synonym for grin.

Practice Circle the word that would come first in a thesaurus.

1. ball (ate) cat

Put the words *ball, ate,* and *cat* in ABC order.

2. a. ate _____

b. ball _____

c. cat _____

Write a word from the box next to its synonyms.

jump	cry	eat

3. gobble, chew, eat _____

4. sob, weep, cry _____

5. leap, spring, jump _____

Name _____ Date _____

▶Review

GRAMMAR AND USAGE

> **Rule**
>
> ▶**Proper nouns** begin with capital letters.
>
> ▶**Subject pronouns** replace subjects in sentences.
>
> ▶**Object pronouns** replace objects in sentences.
>
> ▶**Action verbs** tell what someone is doing.
>
> ▶**Possessive nouns** *and* **pronouns** show ownership

Practice

▶**Underline three times (≡) the letters that should be capitalized.**

1. <u>k</u>imberly baked a cake.

2. We gave the cake to <u>h</u>arold.

▶**Write the action verb in each sentence on the line.**

3. George Washington crossed the river. **crossed**

4. He chopped down a tree. **chopped**

▶**Make these words possessive.**

5. He **His**

6. Adam **Adam's**

▶ Drawing Conclusions

COMPREHENSION

Focus Readers can use information from the writer to draw conclusions about the story.

- To **draw a conclusion**, a reader should use information that a writer gives about a thing, character, or event.
- Conclusions must be supported by information in the story.

Practice Read the information below. Then, draw a line under the conclusion that is best supported by the information.

1. During the summer, many birds build nests and have babies in the north. Birds have a hard time finding food when the weather gets colder. Some birds fly south when they can't find food. Migrate means "to move from one place to another."

   Conclusion A: <u>Birds migrate south for the winter</u>.

   Conclusion B: <u>Birds never migrate</u>.

2. Alfonso couldn't finish his breakfast. He had prepared a speech about the history of his school. Alfonso's knees wobbled when he walked toward the gym. He had never given a speech in front of the whole school before.

▶**Drawing Conclusions**

Conclusion A: <u>Alfonso did not go to gym class.</u>

Conclusion B: <u>Alfonso was nervous about giving a speech at</u>

<u>school.</u>

3. Some men and women are putting up a large tent. A sign next to the booth says, "Circus." A train brought elephants, tigers, and other animals into the station. Acrobats are practicing tricks on a trampoline near the tent.

Conclusion A: <u>The circus is in town.</u>

Conclusion B: <u>The circus is leaving.</u>

Apply **Read the sentences below. Then, draw a conclusion based on the sentences.**

▶ Gardening requires a lot of tools.

▶ It is important to know which flowers and vegetables need a lot of sun.

Answers will vary. Possible answer is shown.

▶ Weeds need to be pulled, and plants need to be watered daily.

▶ Sometimes insects can damage plants.

1. Conclusion: **Gardening is a lot of work and requires**

knowledge of plants.

COMPREHENSION

UNIT 2 Kindness • **Lesson I** *Mushroom in the Rain*

▶ The /a/ Sound

> mat   cap
>
> Say each word and listen for the middle sound. The /a/ sound is spelled *a* in the middle of words.

Spelling Strategies

| dash | ran | map | path | sat |

Consonant Substitution Replace the underlined letter to make a new word. The /a/ sound will be spelled the same.

1. <u>t</u>an   +   r   =   **ran** _____

2. <u>c</u>ap   +   m   =   **map** _____

3. <u>b</u>at   +   s   =   **sat** _____

4. <u>b</u>ash   +   d   =   **dash** _____

5. <u>m</u>ath   +   p   =   **path** _____

▶ **What letter spells /a/ in each word?**

a _____

Name _____ Date _____

Base Word Families

A **base word** is a word that can stand alone.

It gives you a clue to the meaning of other words in its family.

Base Word	Base Word Family Members
rain	raindrop
	raincoat

Write the base word for each pair of words below. The first one is done for you.

1. rub   rubbing   <u>rub</u>

2. snow   snowman   **snow** _____

3. feel   feeling   **feel** _____

4. run   runner   **run** _____

5. big   bigger   **big** _____

6. truck   firetruck   **truck** _____

VOCABULARY

▶Capitalization: Beginnings of Sentences

MECHANICS

Rule	**Example**
▶The first word of *every* sentence is **capitalized**.	▶The library is closed. Did you do your homework? I want to go to the zoo.

Practice Read the following paragraph. Underline the words that should start with a capital letter.

<u>the</u> solar system is made up of the sun and nine planets. <u>the</u> sun is a star and is at the center of the solar system. <u>earth</u> is the third planet from the sun. <u>pluto</u> is the planet farthest away from the sun. <u>did</u> you know that Saturn has rings around it? <u>i</u> want to be an astronaut so I can travel through the solar system.

▶ Tone of a Personal Letter

> Tone tells the writer's feelings.
>
> Use a friendly tone in your personal letters.

Practice   Write *friendly* next to the sentences that have a friendly tone.

1. Thank you for coming to my party.

friendly
_____

2. I don't want you to visit.

_____

3. Please write back soon.

friendly
_____

4. Would you like me to help you?

friendly
_____

5. You should be quiet.

_____

WRITER'S CRAFT

► Sequence

COMPREHENSION

Focus The more you know about the time that things happen in a story and the order in which things happen, the better you can understand the story.

Here are some words that tell the **time** or when things happen.

today, this morning, once upon a time

Here are some words that tell the **order** in which things happen.

first, then, finally

Practice

► Read the sentences. Underline the time or order word or words in each sentence.

1. Let's do our homework. Then, we can play soccer.

2. Today I have a dentist appointment.

3. The last thing to do is to lock the door.

4. Yesterday my dog got loose.

5. Once upon a time, a dragon lived in a cave.

6. This morning I had cereal for breakfast.

UNIT 2   Kindness • **Lesson 2** *The Elves and the Shoemaker*

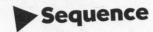 **Sequence**

7. Did you <u>finally</u> get to visit your aunt?

8. <u>Before</u> you leave, please finish your chores.

▶ **Use the words in the box to complete the sentences.**

today	finally	before	earlier	next

Answers will vary.

9. I got up **before** anyone else in my family.

10. Bonnie wanted to be the **next** one to get her picture taken.

11. We are going to the library **today**.

12. Phil said he had seen the lunch box **earlier** in the day.

Apply   **Write a sentence using one of the words or phrases in the box below.**   **Answers will vary.**

tonight	once	the next morning

_____

_____

COMPREHENSION

UNIT 2 Kindness • **Lesson 2** *The Elves and the Shoemaker*

▶ The /e/ Sound

SPELLING

bed   best

Say each word and listen for the middle sound. The /e/ sound is spelled *e* in the middle of words.

Spelling Strategies

nest	bell	yet	fed	then

 Rhyming Strategy Say each pair of words. Write the word from the box that rhymes.

1. fell   tell   <u>**bell**</u>

2. led   bed   <u>**fed**</u>

3. set   wet   <u>**yet**</u>

4. rest   best   <u>**nest**</u>

5. when   hen   <u>**then**</u>

▶ **What letter spells /e/ in each word?**

<u>**e**</u>

▶Homophones

Homophones are words that sound alike. They are not spelled the same and do not have the same meaning.
>   Can you <u>hear</u> the drum?
>   I think the band is <u>here</u>.

Write the word from the box that completes the homophone pair. The first one is done for you.

too	beat	ate	for	blue
know	pear	sew	meat	sun

1. eight   <u>ate</u>

2. blew   **blue**

3. meet   **meat**

4. two   **too**

5. pair   **pear**

6. so   **sew**

7. no   **know**

8. beet   **beat**

9. four   **for**

10. son   **sun**

VOCABULARY

MECHANICS

▶ Commas: Greetings and Closings

Commas are used when writing letters.

Rule	Example
▶ Commas are used in the greeting of a letter.	▶ Dear Mr. President, Dear George,
▶ Commas are used at the closing of a letter.	▶ Sincerely, Owen
	▶ Yours truly, Cho

Practice Read the letter below. Add commas where needed.

Dear Albert,

I enjoyed reading your letter. You must be very smart. Continue to study hard and keep up the good work. I hope to receive more letters from you.

Sincerely,

Max

Name _____ Date _____

▶ Sentence Elaboration

Add details to your sentences to make your writing more interesting.

Example

My rabbit is nice!

With Details: My rabbit is gold and white, and can drink from a cup!

Ask these questions to help you add details.

▶ Did I tell where or when?

▶ Did I put a picture in the reader's mind?

▶ Did I tell why?

Practice **Write words that add detail in each sentence.**

1. Sammy went to visit his grandma.

   Answers will vary _____

2. The mountains are big. ___**Answers will vary**_____

3. I like soccer. __**Answers will vary**_____

4. We were on the road. __**Answers will vary**_____

5. We moved to Denver. __**Answers will vary**_____

UNIT 2 **Kindness • Lesson 3** *The Paper Crane*

▶The /i/ Sound

SPELLING

> rib   trip
>
> Say each word and listen for the middle sound. The /i/ sound is spelled *i* in the middle of words.

Spelling Strategies

zip	win	sit	lips	mix

Pronunciation Strategy Say each pair of words. Write the word from the box that rhymes. Circle the letter that spells /i/ in each word.

1. lit   bit   ___s(i)t___

2. hips   tips   ___l(i)ps___

3. rip   nip   ___z(i)p___

4. pin   bin   ___w(i)n___

5. fix   six   ___m(i)x___

UNIT 2 Kindness • **Lesson 3** *The Paper Crane*

▶ Levels of Specificity Categories

A **category** is a group of similar things. Different types of things can be in the same category.

| mouse pigs crayon book pencil elephant |

Which words belong in the **animal** category? **Order of answers will vary.**

1. mouse

3. pigs

2. elephant

Which of these animals is the smallest?

4. mouse

Which of these animals is the biggest?

5. elephant

Which words belong in the **things at school** category?

6. book

8. crayon

7. pencil

Which of these things can you write with?

9. pencil

10. crayon

VOCABULARY

UNIT 2 Kindness • **Lesson 3** *The Paper Crane*

▶ Capitalization: Names of days, months, and greetings of letters

MECHANICS

Rule	Example
▶ The names of **days** and **months** are capitalized.	▶ Tuesday Saturday December March
▶ The first word in the **greeting** of a letter is capitalized.	▶ Dear Kelsey,

Practice Rewrite the following words or greetings on the line with the proper capitalization.

1. wednesday **Wednesday** _____

2. january **January** _____

3. april **April** _____

4. dear Enrique **Dear Enrique** _____

5. thursday **Thursday** _____

Capitalization: Names of days, months, and greetings of letters • **Reteach**

▶ Structure of a Personal Letter

Your personal letter should have these five parts.

1. Heading
2. Greeting
3. Body
4. Closing
5. Your name

 **Practice** **Write a letter to a friend about your favorite subject.**

Heading
_____

Greeting
_____

Body
_____

_____

_____

Closing
_____

Your Name
_____

WRITER'S CRAFT

▶The /o/ and /aw/ Sounds

dog   lot

Say each word and listen for the middle sound. The /o/ and /aw/ sounds are spelled *o* in the middle of words.

SPELLING

Spelling Strategies

| fog | cot | flop | drops | long |

Rhyming Strategy Say each pair of words. Write the word from the box that rhymes with each pair of words.

1. tops   mops   **drops** _____

2. jog   log   **fog** _____

3. lot   dot   **cot** _____

4. song   gong   **long** _____

5. plop   stop   **flop** _____

▶**Which letter spells /o/ and /aw/ in each word?**

o _____

Name _____ Date _____

▶ Multiple Meanings

Some words have more than one meaning.
> *Trail* may mean "follow" or "path"
> *Blue* may mean "a color" or "sad"
> *Spot* may mean: "to see" or "a place"

You need to look at the words around these words to
know what they mean.

**Use the underlined clue to figure out the meaning of a
word. Then write the meaning of the word.**

1. The <u>sad</u> child was blue because he lost his puppy.

   blue means: **sad** _____

2. Can you <u>see</u> the airplane? I can't spot it.

   spot means: **see** _____

3. The <u>colors</u> on the flag were blue, white, and red.

   blue means: **a color** _____

4. This spot is perfect for a picnic. It is a flat <u>place</u>.

   spot means: **place** _____

5. The dog walked on the trail, sniffing the <u>path</u>.

   trail means: **path** _____

VOCABULARY

▶ Commas: Words in a Series

MECHANICS

Rule	**Example**
▶ A **comma** is used after each item in a list. The comma helps to separate the items when we read. This makes reading a list easier.	▶ Tyrone went to the store to buy milk, bread, potatoes, cereal, and cheese. I have to remember to bring my glove, bat, ball, and hat to baseball practice.

Practice **Read the following sentences. Add commas where they are needed.**

1. Sylvia packed her sleeping bag, tent, clothes, and toothbrush for her camping trip.

2. Allan's favorite subjects are English, science, and math.

3. Tameka felt happy, rested, and silly after camp.

4. Harlan rode on a tractor, horse, and a truck at the farm.

5. The four oceans are the Pacific, Atlantic, Indian, and Arctic.

Name _____ Date _____

▶ Time and Order Words

Time words tell when something happens.
Order words tell the order that things happen.

Practice Finish each sentence with a time or order word from the box.

next	yesterday	finally	today	first

1. __Yesterday_____, our class went to a park.

2. __First_____, we went on a nature hike.

3. __Next_____, we learned about plants and trees.

4. __Finally_____, we learned about insects.

5. __Today_____, our class took a test on plants and trees.

WRITER'S CRAFT

► Making Inferences

COMPREHENSION

Focus Sometimes a writer does not tell the reader everything. Readers must use what they already know to understand the story.

Readers can use what they already know to figure out details the author left out.

Here is an example.

Kelley grabbed her bat and glove and hurried to the park.

I know that a bat and glove are used in playing baseball and softball, so Kelley must be going to play ball at the park.

Practice Read each sentence below. Write clues from the sentence that tell what happened. Then write what the clue tells you. The first one is done for you.
Answers may vary. Possible answers are shown.

1. Juan was so excited he couldn't sleep. He got up before the alarm went off and checked his suitcase again.

   Clue: <u>Juan was so excited he couldn't sleep.</u>

   Clue: <u>He got up and checked his suitcase.</u>

   What the clues tell you: <u>Juan must be going on a trip.</u>

▶**Making Inferences**

2. The balloons were tied to the door. The table was set for ten, and there were party hats by each place. There was a table for presents by the door.

Clue: **There were balloons and party hats.**

Clue: **There was a table for presents**

What the clues tell you: **There is going to be a birthday party.**

3. The dog wagged his tail as he looked out the window. He barked and ran to the door.

Clue: **The dog wagged his tail and barked.**

Clue: **The dog ran to the door.**

What the clues tell you: **The dog sees someone coming to the house.**

4. All of the boxes were in the truck. Sally locked the front door. She got in the truck and sadly looked at the house as they drove away.

Clue: **There was a truck with boxes.**

Clue: **Sally locked up the house.**

What the clues tell you: **Sally is sad she is moving.**

COMPREHENSION

UNIT 2 Kindness • **Lesson 5** *Corduroy*

▶ The /u/ Sound

SPELLING

luck   tug
Say each word and listen for the middle sound. The /u/ sound is spelled *u* in the middle of words.

Spelling Strategies

hug   **rust**   **duck**   **mud**   **shut**

 Rhyming Strategy Say each pair of words. Write the word from the box that rhymes. Underline the letter that spells /u/ in each word.

1. hut   but   sh<u>u</u>t _____

2. bud   dud   m<u>u</u>d _____

3. rug   tug   h<u>u</u>g _____

4. must   just   r<u>u</u>st _____

5. luck   stuck   d<u>u</u>ck _____

▶Homographs

> **Homographs** are words that have the same spelling, but different pronunciations and meanings.
>   *wind* may mean "blowing air" or "wrap around"
>   *does* may mean "female deer" or "is doing"

Say the homograph and write its meaning.

Say *wind* so that it rhymes with *pinned*.

1. The wind blew my kite high in the sky.

wind means ___**blowing air**___

Say *does* so that it rhymes with *toes*.

2. The does ate the new, green grass.

does means ___**female deer**___

Say *does* so that it rhymes with *because*.

3. He does his homework when he gets home.

does means ___**is doing**___

VOCABULARY

▶ Quotation Marks and Underlining

Rule	Example
▶ **Quotation marks** are used to show the words of a speaker. They are used at the beginning and end of the speaker's words.	▶ "I got an A on the spelling test," said Rafael.
▶ **Quotation marks** are used for the title of a story, poem, or the chapter of a book.	▶ I like the story "Hansel and Gretel."
▶ **Underline** the title of a book or movie.	▶ <u>Cinderella</u> is Rosa's favorite movie.

Practice

▶ **Read the following. Add quotation marks.**

1. "The Mississippi River starts in Canada," said George.

▶ **Read the following. Add quotation marks or underlining.**

2. <u>Pinocchio</u> is my favorite movie.

3. "A Christmas Carol" is a story by Charles Dickens.

UNIT 2   Kindness • **Lesson 5** *Corduroy*

▶ Sensory Details

WRITER'S CRAFT

Rule

Sensory details make a picture in the reader's mind. These words help readers **see, hear, feel, smell,** or **taste** things.

Example

Here are some examples.

| red | loud | soft | sweet | bitter |

Practice   **Say whether each underlined word tells about seeing, hearing, feeling, smelling, or tasting.**

1. The snow was <u>cold</u>. feeling _____

2. My dad's coffee is <u>bitter</u>. tasting _____

3. The tree is <u>tall</u> and green. seeing _____

4. Ben plays <u>loud</u> music. hearing _____

5. The eggs gave off a <u>rotten</u> odor. smelling _____

▶ The Final /ən/ Sound

SPELLING

chicken   cabin   person

Say each word and listen for the final sound. The final /ən/ sound is spelled *en*, *in*, and *on* at the end of words.

Spelling Strategies

seven   wagon   robin   open   broken

 Meaning Strategy Complete each sentence with a word from the box.

1. The opposite of closed is _____**open**_____.

2. My crayon was _____**broken**_____ in two.

3. The little red _____**wagon**_____ had four wheels.

4. A week has _____**seven**_____ days.

5. The finch and the _____**robin**_____ are birds.

UNIT 2 Kindness • **Lesson 6** *The Story of Three Whales*

▶ Shades of Meaning

Words can have strengths that make them different. We can show this by ranking words on a scale from 1 to 10.

                    1 . . . . 5 10

Example: warm   hot   burning

Can you see that *hot* has a different strength than *warm?*

scream	cool	sip	shove	bite

Complete the shades of meaning ranges below with words from the box.

1. tap   nudge   <u>**shove**</u>

2. nibble   <u>**bite**</u>   gobble

3. <u>**cool**</u>   cold   frozen

4. <u>**sip**</u>   drink   gulp

5. whisper   speak   <u>**scream**</u>

VOCABULARY

UNIT 2 Kindness • **Lesson 6** *The Story of Three Whales*

MECHANICS

▶ Commas: Cities, States, and Dates

Rule
- ▶ A **comma** is used between the name of a city and state.

- ▶ A **comma** is used between the day and the year.

Example
- ▶ Columbus, Ohio
  San Francisco, California

- ▶ May 15, 2001
  July 27, 2002

Practice Rewrite the following dates and cities. Add commas where necessary.

1. September 17 1995 **September 17, 1995** _____

2. Chicago Illinois **Chicago, Illinois** _____

3. Dallas Texas **Dallas, Texas** _____

4. January 8 1993 **January 8, 1993** _____

5. February 14 2005 **February 14, 2005** _____

Name _____ Date _____

▶ Structure of a Business Letter

A business letter has six parts.
1. Heading: Your address and date.
2. Inside Address: Name and address of the person to whom you are writing.
3. Greeting: *Dear* and the person's name to whom you are writing.
4. Body: Tell what you want.
5. Closing: *Sincerely* or *Thank You.*
6. Signature: Write your first and last name.

WRITER'S CRAFT

Practice   **Write a business letter to your local library to ask for a library card.**

Heading _____

Inside Address _____

Greeting _____

Body _____

_____

_____

Closing _____

Your Name _____

UNIT 2 Kindness • **Lesson 7** *Cinderella*

▶Review

| b<u>e</u>st | p<u>i</u>g | h<u>o</u>t | m<u>u</u>sh |

Say each word and listen for the middle sound. The underlined letters all spell short-vowel sounds.

SPELLING

Spelling Strategies

| **bend** | **dog** | **rush** | **milk** | **has** |

Visualization Strategy Circle the correctly spelled word. Then write the word.

1. (has)   hase   **has** _____

2. binde   (bend)   **bend** _____

3. melk   (milk)   **milk** _____

4. (rush)   ruch   **rush** _____

5. (log)   loge   **log** _____

▶Review

Homophones are words that sound alike. They are not spelled the same and do not have the same meaning.

Homographs are words that have the same spelling, but different pronunciations and meanings.

to   wind   two   too   does

▶ **Write the three words from the box that are homophones.**

1. to _____

2. two _____

3. too _____

▶ **Write the word that rhymes with *because* or *nose*.**

4. does _____

▶ **Write the word that rhymes with *find* or *pinned*.**

5. wind _____

wind and *does* are __homographs_____

VOCABULARY

UNIT 2 Kindness • **Lesson 7** *Cinderella*

▶Unit Review

MECHANICS

> **Rule**
>
> ▶ The first word of a sentence is **capitalized**.
>
> ▶ The *names* of **days** and **months** are capitalized.
>
> ▶ **Commas** are used in the greeting and closing of a letter.
>
> ▶ A **comma** is used after each item in a list.
>
> ▶ A **comma** is used between the name of a city and state.
>
> ▶ A **comma** is also used between the day and the year when writing a date.
>
> ▶ **Quotation marks** are used to show the words of a speaker.
>
> ▶ **Underlining** is used to show the title of a book or movie.

Practice Correct the following sentences.

1. wilson borrowed Little House on the Prairie from the library.

   Wilson borrowed <u>Little House on the Prairie</u> from the

   library.

2. please bring a coat hat and scarf to Hillary's party on January 12 2003, said Mrs. Chan.

   "Please bring a coat, hat, and scarf to Hillary's party on

   January 12, 2003," said Mrs. Chan.

▶Background Information

Make sure you tell your reader facts about what you are writing.

Be sure to give background information about

▶ People

▶ Places

▶ Events

Ask yourself what the reader needs to know about your topic.

   **Write a paragraph with background information about yourself. You could write about your family, where you live, or what you like to do.**

Answers will vary

_____

_____

_____

_____

_____

_____

WRITER'S CRAFT

▶The /ā/Sound

The /ā/ sound sounds like the name of the letter *a*. It can be spelled

a_e with a silent *e*	n<u>a</u>m<u>e</u>
ay at the end of word	pl<u>ay</u>
ai in the middle of a word	t<u>ai</u>l

pail	**way**	**came**	**snake**	**wait**

 Meaning Strategy
Write the word from the box that rhymes with each pair of words.

1. name   same   <u>came</u>

2. play   stay   <u>way</u>

3. take   rake   <u>snake</u>

4. tail   sail   <u>pail</u>

5. bait   trait   <u>wait</u>

SPELLING

UNIT 3 Look Again • **Lesson I** *I See Animals Hiding*

▶Base Word Families

> A **base word** is a word that can stand alone.
>
> It gives you a clue to the meaning of other words in its family.
>
> | **Base Word** | **Base Word Family Members** |
> |---|---|
> | bird | birdbath |
> | | songbird |

Circle the words that belong to the same base word family. Then underline the base word. The first one is done for you.

1. (<u>fishing</u>)   fanned   (<u>fished</u>)

2. flatter   (<u>faster</u>)   (<u>fastest</u>)

3. (<u>bikes</u>)   (<u>bikers</u>)   beak

4. (<u>anthill</u>)   (<u>anteater</u>)   paints

5. (<u>kinder</u>)   kids   (un<u>kind</u>)

6. (<u>walking</u>)   winking   (<u>walked</u>)

VOCABULARY

▶ Kinds of Sentences

GRAMMAR AND USAGE

Rule	Example
▶ **Declarative sentences** make a statement and end in a period (.).	▶ Earth is round.
▶ **Interrogative sentences** ask a question and end in a question mark (?).	▶ Is Earth round?
▶ **Imperative sentences** give a command and end in a period (.).	▶ Take out the trash.
▶ **Exclamatory sentences** show great feeling or emotion and end in an exclamation point (!).	▶ Tracie, take out the trash now!

Practice   **Write what kind of sentence each is on the line.**

1. Friction is a topic we studied in science. ___declarative___

2. What is friction? ___interrogative___

3. Friction is a force caused by two things rubbing

   together. ___declarative___

                                                     exclamatory

4. Without friction you couldn't walk! _____

5. Your feet push against the ground when you walk

   causing friction. ___declarative___

▶Organizing Expository Writing

▶ Expository writing gives facts.

▶ Organize your details with the most important facts first.

▶ You can also put details in the order in which things happen.

Practice **Write these sentences in the correct order.**

Mix the ingredients.

Preheat the oven.

Put eggs, sugar, and flour in a bowl.

Put it in the oven for one hour.

Put the mixture in a pan.

Preheat the oven.
_____

Put eggs, sugar, and flour in a bowl.
_____

Mix the ingredients.
_____

Put the mixture in a pan.
_____

Put it in the oven for one hour.

WRITER'S CRAFT

UNIT 3 Look Again • **Lesson I** *I See Animals Hiding*

▶ Topic Sentences

WRITER'S CRAFT

> A topic sentence tells the main idea of a paragraph. You
> can put your topic sentence at the beginning of the
> paragraph.
>
> **Example**
>
> <u>Fish make great pets</u>. They do not cost a lot. Fish are easy
> to feed. It is fun to watch them swim.

Practice Write a topic sentence that goes with these details.

Possible answer: Making a peanut butter sandwich
_____

is easy.
_____

1. First, put the peanut butter on one slice of bread.

2. Next, put your favorite jelly on the other slice
   of the bread.

3. Last, put the two slices of bread together.

Drawing Conclusions

COMPREHENSION

Focus

> ▶ To **draw a conclusion**, a reader should use information that a writer gives about a thing, character, or event.
>
> ▶ Conclusions must be supported by the information in the story.

Practice

Read each paragraph. Then, draw a conclusion by answering the question.

We made sandwiches and put ice in the cooler. Mother packed lemonade, homemade cookies, cups, and napkins. Our beach towels and chairs were in the car. The sand toys were packed, too. Each of us had on our bathing suit.

Answers will vary. Possible answers are shown.

Where do you think the people are going?

These people are going to the beach or a pool.

The day we arrived was perfect. We saw the ocean and walked on the beach. The sunset was beautiful. The next day we visited the local zoo. It will be hard to go home again on Saturday.

Where are these people?

These people are on vacation.

▶**Drawing Conclusions**

COMPREHENSION

The cars and taxis honked. People walked quickly, carrying packages and briefcases. Traffic lights changed, buses dropped people off, and police officers blew their whistles.

Where does this story take place?

This story takes place in a big city.

 Read the sentences. Then, use what they tell you to answer the question.

▶ The two slides were shining in the sun.

▶ The swings were empty.

▶ The merry-go-round had a father and son on it.

▶ The see-saw was still.

Answers will vary. Possible answers are shown.

1. Where does this take place?

at a park

▶ Begin floating by pushing away from the wall.

▶ Kick your feet.

▶ Cup your hands as you paddle with your arms.

▶ Put your face in the water part of the time.

2. What are you doing?

swimming

▶The /ē/ Sound

The /ē/ sound sounds like the name of the letter *e*. It can be spelled

ea	dr<u>ea</u>m
e_e with a silent *e*	th<u>e</u>s<u>e</u>
ee	tr<u>ee</u>
y at the end of a word	happ<u>y</u>

sneak	**silly**	**feet**	**green**	**team**

Rhyming Strategy
Write the word from the box that rhymes with each pair of words.

1. seen   teen   <u>**green**</u>

2. filly   chilly   <u>**silly**</u>

3. beak   leak   <u>**sneak**</u>

4. dream   steam   <u>**team**</u>

5. greet   meet   <u>**feet**</u>

SPELLING

▶ Prefixes

A **prefix** is added to the beginning of a word. The prefix *over-* can change a word to mean "too much."

over + eat = "eat too much"

A child may <u>overeat</u> if he is given ice cream.

▶ **Add the prefix *over-*, then write what the word means. The first one is done for you.**

1. over   +   cooked =   overcooked

   meaning: cooked too much

2. over   +   did   =   **overdid**

   meaning: **did too much**

The prefix *un-* can change a word to mean "not."

Un   +   kind   =   "not kind"

The girl was <u>unkind</u>, and did not share her ice cream.

▶ **Add the prefix *un-*, then write what the word means.**

3. un   +   fair   =   **unfair**

   meaning: **not fair**

VOCABULARY

▶Linking Verbs and Helping Verbs

GRAMMAR AND USAGE

Practice

Rule	**Example**
▶**Linking verbs** join or connect parts of sentences to make them complete. Linking verbs *don't* show action.	▶Roland **is** a volleyball player. ▶Carlos **was** a baker.
▶**Helping verbs** are used with action verbs to help tell when something is happening.	▶The girls **were** playing baseball. ▶The boys **are** walking on the field.

Practice
Read the following sentences. Write *linking* or *helping* on the line.

1. Elizabeth Dole <u>was</u> president of the Red Cross.   _linking_

2. Gloria <u>is</u> hoping to be president.   _helping_

3. Bill Clinton <u>was</u> president.   _linking_

4. Someone <u>is</u> always president.   _linking_

5. The President <u>was</u> traveling the country.   _helping_

WRITER'S CRAFT

▶ Note Taking

Take good notes to help you remember facts.

Tips:

▶ Make headings. You may have many facts under one heading.

▶ Write your notes in your own words.

▶ Write only important facts.

▶ Write neatly.

Practice **Underline the most important facts.**

The ostrich is the largest bird. It grows up to 8 feet tall. It weighs 250–350 pounds. It has a very long neck and long legs. Ostriches do not fly, but they can run fast. They can run up to 40 miles per hour. They eat mostly plants.

▶The /ī/ Sound

The /ī/ sound sounds like the name of the letter *i*. It can be
spelled: hi̱   mi̱le̱   pi̱e̱   sky̱   hi̱gẖ

pie	night	find	fly	tie

Consonant-Substitution Strategy
Change the letter or letters to make a word
from the box. The spelling of the /ī/ sound will
stay the same.

1. ṟight   +   n   =   <u>night</u>

2. ḏie   +   p   =   <u>pie</u>

3. ḇy   +   fl   =   <u>fly</u>

4. ḻie   +   t   =   <u>tie</u>

5. m̱ind   +   f   =   <u>find</u>

SPELLING

▶ Compound Words

VOCABULARY

> A **compound word** is a word made from two words.
> moon　　+　　light　　=　　moonlight

Read each sentence. Circle the word that will correctly complete the compound word and write it on the line.

1. The nest was built by a blue [bird]_____.　　(bird)　　berry

2. A rider rode on horse [back]_____.　　shoe　　(back)

3. The kicker kicked the foot [ball]_____.　　step　　(ball)

4. The rain [bow]_____ had pretty colors.　　storm　　(bow)

5. The snow [man]_____ had a button nose.　　flake　　(man)

▶ Subject/Verb Agreement

The subject and verb of a sentence must agree.

Rule	**Example**
▶ A **singular subject** must have a **singular verb.**	▶ An **owl changes** its color. (owl=singular subject, changes=singular verb)
▶ A **plural subject** must have a **plural verb.**	▶ The **owls change** their color. (owls=plural subject, change=plural verb)

Practice

▶ **Underline the correct verb to complete each sentence.**

1. Tadpoles (<u>grow</u>, grows) into frogs.

2. Moles (<u>dig</u>, digs) tunnels in the ground.

3. The bat (hang, <u>hangs</u>) upside-down.

▶ **Underline the subject. Circle the verb. Write *singular* or *plural* on the line.**

4. The <u>bear</u> (hibernates) in the winter.   singular

5. The <u>birds</u> (build) a nest.   plural

6. The <u>bluebird</u> (flies) south for the winter.   singular

▶ Transition Words

WRITER'S CRAFT

Transition words help readers know when and how things happen. They can tell time and order.

Transition Words:

first	next	then	later
last	finally	in the beginning	

Practice Finish these sentences with the correct transition words from the box.

then	finally	first	later	next

1. <u>**First**</u>, we got out our bikes.

2. <u>**Next**</u>, we rode to the park.

3. <u>**Then**</u>, we rode past the school.

4. <u>**Finally**</u>, we went back home.

5. <u>**Later**</u>, we will ride to the playground.

▶The /ō/ Sound

> The /ō/ sound sounds like the name of the letter *o*. It can be spelled: s<u>o</u> kn<u>ow</u> j<u>o</u>k<u>e</u> b<u>oa</u>t f<u>oe</u>

coat	toe	poke	blow	note

Visualization Strategy
Circle the correctly spelled word. Then write the word.

1. noet   (note)   **note** _____

2. pok   (poke)   **poke** _____

3. (coat)   coet   **coat** _____

4. teo   (toe)   **toe** _____

5. (blow)   bloe   **blow** _____

SPELLING

▶ Suffixes

A **suffix** is added to the end of a word. The suffix **-er** changes a word so that it means "more."

tall   +   er   =   "more tall"

The father is <u>taller</u> than his son.

Draw a line from the word with *-er* added to the words that tell what it means.

1. <u>warmer</u>   more quiet

2. <u>softer</u>   more warm

3. <u>quieter</u>   more kind

4. <u>meaner</u>   more light

5. <u>harder</u>   more mean

6. <u>lighter</u>   more soft

7. <u>kinder</u>   more hard

VOCABULARY

▶ Parts of a Sentence

Sentences must have a **subject** and a **predicate** to be complete.

Rule

▶ The subject tells who or what the sentence is about.

▶ The predicate tells what the subject *is* or *does*.

Example

▶ **Jean** is my best friend.

▶ **My oldest brother** is going to college.

▶ Jean **is my best friend.**

▶ My oldest brother **is going to college.**

 Practice   **Read each sentence. Draw a line under the subject and circle the predicate.**

1. <u>Dinosaurs</u> (lived many million years ago.)

2. <u>No one</u> (knows why the dinosaurs died.)

3. <u>Some scientists</u> (think a huge meteorite hit Earth.)

4. <u>It</u> (probably caused a large cloud of dust.)

5. <u>The dust</u> (blocked the sun's light.)

6. <u>Earth</u> (became dark and the climate changed.)

7. <u>The dinosaurs</u> (could not adapt to the changes.)

GRAMMAR AND USAGE

▶ Organizing Expository Writing

WRITER'S CRAFT

▶ Expository writing gives facts.

▶ Organize your details with the most important facts first.

▶ You can also put details in the order in which things happen.

Practice **Write these sentences in the correct order.**

He got a home run.

He ran around the bases.

It was Josh's turn to bat.

He hit the ball.

He waited for the pitch.

It was Josh's turn to bat.
_____

He waited for the pitch.
_____

He hit the ball.
_____

He ran around the bases.
_____

He got a home run.
_____

Supporting Details

> • **A main idea** is the topic of the paragraph.
> • **Supporting details** tell about the main idea.

Practice Draw lines from the main ideas to the details that go with them.

Main Ideas	Details

Playing in a band is fun.

–Musicians like to work together to play music.

–Bands often march in parades.

The city streets are busy.

–Cars dart in and out of traffic lanes.

–Crowds of people walk the streets.

–Learning to play an instrument is fun.

–Horns blow, engines race, and people shout.

WRITER'S CRAFT

COMPREHENSION

▶ Classify and Categorize

Focus   Readers classify and categorize to help keep track of information in a story.

Here is one way to **classify** information.

▶ Name the categories or kinds of things, characters, or events. For example,

Art Supplies   **School Supplies**

▶ List the things, characters, or events that fit under each category. For example,

Art Supplies   **School Supplies**
crayons, paints,   scissors, pencils,
scissors, brushes   papers, crayons

Sometimes things, characters, or events can fit into more than one category. Such as *scissors* and *crayons* for the two categories above.

Practice   Circle the thing that does not fit into the category.

1. Things to play with

   balls   (stores)   dolls   games

2. Things to eat

   apples   carrots   (lamps)   potatoes

UNIT 3 **Look Again • Lesson 5** *How the Guinea Fowl Got Her Spots*

▶**Classify and Categorize**

3. Things with wheels

(dogs)   bikes   cars   trucks

4. Things that drink water

people   cats   dogs   (books)

5. Parts of a bird

head   (hands)   beak   wings

6. School supplies

pencil   paper   crayon   (hammer)

 **Apply** Look at the things in the box. List each thing under the correct category.

| toothpaste | plates | shampoo | napkins |
| toothbrush | comb | forks | pots |

Things you might find in a bathroom

toothbrush

shampoo

comb

toothpaste

Things you might find in a kitchen

plates

napkins

forks

pots

COMPREHENSION

▶ The /o͞o/ Sound

SPELLING

> Say the word *moo*. This word has the /o͞o/ sound. The /o͞o/ sound can be spelled: n<u>oo</u>n   d<u>u</u>n<u>e</u>   d<u>ew</u>   d<u>o</u>

tune	toot	moon	knew	room

 Rhyming Strategy
Write the word from the box that rhymes. This word will have the same spelling of the /o͞o/ sound.

1. gloom   doom   **room** _____

2. new   blew   **knew** _____

3. loot   hoot   **toot** _____

4. prune   dune   **tune** _____

5. soon   noon   **moon** _____

▶Suffixes

A *suffix* is added to the end of a word. The suffix *-ly* changes a word so that it means "in a certain way."

loud   +   ly   =   "in a loud way"

The music <u>loudly</u> boomed from the radio.

Add the suffix *-ly*, then write what the word means.

1. slow   +   ly   = <u>slowly</u>

meaning: <u>in a slow way</u>

2. nice   +   ly   = <u>nicely</u>

meaning: <u>in a nice way</u>

3. kind   +   ly   = <u>kindly</u>

meaning: <u>in a kind way</u>

4. quick   +   ly   = <u>quickly</u>

meaning: <u>in a quick way</u>

5. quiet   +   ly   = <u>quietly</u>

meaning: <u>in a quiet way</u>

VOCABULARY

UNIT 3 Look Again • **Lesson 5** *How the Guinea Fowl Got Her Spots*

▶ Complete Sentences

Rule

▶ A **complete sentence** has a subject, a predicate, and expresses a complete thought.

▶ A **run-on sentence** is one sentence that should be two.

▶ A **sentence fragment** is not a complete sentence. It is missing either a subject or a predicate.

Example
(subject) (predicate)
▶ Jeremy <u>ate dinner at home</u>.

▶ **Wrong:** The field was muddy he could not run to first base.

▶ **Correct:** The field was muddy. He could not run to first base.

▶ **Wrong:** A yellow bird.

▶ **Correct:** A yellow bird flew in our backyard.

Practice Rewrite the following as a complete sentence.

1. The sky is blue the sun is yellow.

   The sky is blue. The sun is yellow.
   _____

Name _____ Date _____

▶ Place and Location Words

> ▶ Place and location words tell where something is.

Practice **Read the sentences. Underline the place and location words.**

1. I sat <u>beside</u> my friend.

2. Please look over <u>here</u>.

3. Do you want to play <u>outside</u>?

4. Kevin was <u>near</u> the park when the rain started.

5. The keys are <u>under</u> the cushion.

6. Will you sit <u>next to</u> me at lunch?

7. The birds fly <u>above</u> the clouds.

8. Your books are <u>on</u> the desk.

9. The car was <u>inside</u> the garage.

10. The tree is <u>in front of</u> the house.

WRITER'S CRAFT

▶ # Main Idea

Focus Writers use a main idea to tell readers what a paragraph is about.

> ▶ A **main-idea sentence** gives the main idea of a paragraph. The others sentences in the paragraph give details about the main idea.
>
> ▶ Often, the main-idea sentence comes first in a paragraph. Having the main idea sentence first helps readers know what the paragraph will be about.

Practice Read the paragraphs below. Underline the main-idea sentence in each one.

COMPREHENSION

1. <u>Debra's favorite season is winter</u>. She loves to play in the snow and ice skate. In the mornings, she likes the way the frozen ground crunches under her feet. Sometimes her mother makes her hot chocolate for a treat.

2. <u>Saturday is a busy day in my town</u>. Many people start their day at the farmer's market or the bakery. Then, lots of people go to the movies or play at the park.

3. <u>Farming is hard work</u>. The animals need to be fed and let out of the barn. There is always planting or harvesting to be done. Farmers must milk the cows and do other chores, too.

▶**Main Idea**

 Read each paragraph. The main idea is missing. Draw a line under the best main-idea sentence from the box.

Shalene stirs the vegetable soup. It is Grandma's favorite. Shalene adds some pepper to the soup. Then, she sets the table for three—her dad, herself, and Grandma.

Shalene is a good cook.

Dinner with Shalene is always fun.

<u>Grandma is coming for dinner.</u>

Moira found some long dresses at a thrift shop. She added feathers, buttons, and shiny ribbons to the long dresses. They were perfect for the scene in the grand ballroom!

Moira is in the class play.

<u>Moira is in charge of the costumes for our class play.</u>

Moira plays the violin.

COMPREHENSION

▶ Review

rake	deep	shy	snow

 Rhyming Strategy
Say each letter name. Write the word from the box that has the same sound as the letter name. Then think of and write one more word for each sound.

1. *a*   rake _____

2. *e*   deep _____

3. *i*   shy _____

4. *o*   snow _____

Name _____ Date _____

 # Suffixes

A **suffix** is added to the end of a word. The suffix *-est* changes a word so that it means "most."

soft   +   est   =   "most soft"

The poodle was the <u>softest</u> dog I ever felt.

Add the suffix -est, then write what the word means. The first one is done for you.

1. great   +   est   = greatest

meaning: most great

2. high   +   est   = __highest__

meaning: __most high__

3. long   +   est   = __longest__

meaning: __most long__

4. low   +   est   = __lowest__

meaning: __most low__

5. sharp   +   est   = __sharpest__

meaning: __most sharp__

VOCABULARY

▶Review

GRAMMAR AND USAGE

Rule

▸ The **subject** tells who or what the sentence is about.

▸ The **predicate** tells what the subject is or does.

▸ **Run-on sentences** are one sentence that should be two.

Rule

▸ **Sentence fragments** are missing a subject or a predicate.

▸ **Linking verbs** connect parts of sentences.

▸ **Helping verbs** are used with action verbs.

Practice

▶Underline the subject and circle the predicate.

1. The state of Florida (is a peninsula.)

▶Circle the linking or helping verb.

2. The Atlantic Ocean (is) on the east coast of Florida.

▶Write a complete sentence.

3. the big wave Answers will vary. _____

Name _____ Date _____

▶Fact and Opinion

> ▶A **fact** can be proven to be true.
>
> ▶An **opinion** cannot be proven. It is a person's idea.

Practice Read each topic. Then write one sentence that tells a fact. Then write one sentence that tells an opinion about each topic.

WRITER'S CRAFT

1. Topic: School

   Fact: __**Answers will vary**__

   Opinion: __**Answers will vary**__

2. Topic: Basketball

   Fact: __**Answers will vary**__

   Opinion: __**Answers will vary**__

3. Topic: Friends

   Fact: __**Answers will vary**__

   Opinion: __**Answers will vary**__

▶ Words with *wh* and *sh*

SPELLING

Say the words *why* and *shy*. The letters at the beginning of these words combine to make one sound.

shine	why	while	what	shore

Vowel-Substitution Strategy
Replace the underlined vowel sounds to make a new word. This word will begin with the same sound.

1. wh<u>a</u>le   +   i   =   while

2. sh<u>a</u>re   +   o   =   shore

3. wh<u>o</u>   +   y   =   why

4. sh<u>o</u>ne   +   i   =   shine

5. wh<u>ea</u>t   +   a   =   what

UNIT 4 Fossils • **Lesson I** *Fossils Tell of Long Ago*

▶Concept Words

A **concept word** gives a name to an idea. Look for words that tell about a hard concept to discover its meaning.

Circle the words that describe each concept word.

1. gardening

(plants)　　fish　　(soil)　　bananas　　(weeds)

2. weather

(clouds)　(wind)　　grass　(warmth)　　trees

3. energy

(power)　　potatoes　(sunlight)　dogs　　(work)

VOCABULARY

UNIT 4 Fossils • **Lesson I** *Fossils Tell of Long Ago*

► Adjectives

Rule	**Example**
► An **adjective** describes or tells more about a noun or pronoun. Adjectives tell *how many, how much, what color,* or *what kind.*	► He liked a **red** coat. ► Amy ate the **last** apple.
► There are three **articles**: *a, an,* and *the.* Articles are used before a noun.	► **A** banana ► **The** basket

Practice

► **Underline each adjective.**

1. Deer have <u>white</u> tails.

2. There are <u>three</u> eagles in the tree.

3. The <u>wrinkly</u> elephants walked in the jungle.

► **Circle the articles in the sentences below.**

4. Ⓐ black bear stole our food.

5. Ⓣⓗⓔ monkey ate ⓣⓗⓔ banana.

6. Ⓣⓗⓔ bluebird sat on ⓐ fence.

▶ Fact and Opinion

Focus Writers use facts and opinions to support ideas in their writing.

> ▶ A **fact** is a statement that can be proven true.
> Saturn is a planet in our solar system. (You can prove this statement by finding Saturn on a map of the solar system in your science book.)
>
> ▶ An **opinion** is what someone feels or believes is true. An opinion cannot be proven true or false.
> Saturn would be fun to visit. (This statement cannot be proven true or false. It is a statement about what someone believes.)

Practice

▶ **Read the following sentences. Ask yourself the question "Can this sentence be proven true?" If it can be proven true, then it is a fact. Write an *X* next to each sentence that is a fact.**

1. __X__ Five times five is twenty-five.

2. ____ Basketball is more fun than soccer.

3. ____ My brother should buy a red car.

4. __X__ A giraffe is a mammal.

COMPREHENSION

▶**Fact and Opinion**

COMPREHENSION

5. __X__ A grocery store is where people buy food.

6. ____ Triangles are better than circles.

▶**Read the following sentences. Ask yourself the question "Can this sentence be proven true or false?" If it cannot be proven true or false, then it is an opinion. Write an *O* next to each sentence that is an opinion.**

7. ____ A football field is 100 yards long.

8. __O__ Shirts with collars are better than shirts without collars.

9. ____ Rome is in Italy.

10. __O__ Only yellow flowers should be planted in gardens.

11. ____ A bullfighter teases the bull by waving a red cape.

12. __O__ Everyone should eat hot dogs on Sunday.

Apply

▶**What's your opinion about dinosaurs? Write a sentence stating your opinion.**

Answers will vary.

▶**Write a sentence giving one fact that you have learned about dinosaurs.**

Answers will vary.

UNIT 4 Fossils • **Lesson 2** *The Dinosaur Who Lived in My Backyard*

▶Words with *ch* and *th*

Say the words *chin* and *thin*. The letters at the beginning of these words combine to make one sound.

chick	peach	thick	they	thin

Meaning Strategy
Complete each sentence with a word from the box. Then read the sentence aloud.

1. The opposite of thick is <u>thin</u>.

2. A fruit with a pit is a <u>peach</u>.

3. The milkshake was yummy and <u>thick</u>.

4. Don't walk where <u>they</u> did.

5. The <u>chick</u> came out of the egg.

SPELLING

▶Synonyms

VOCABULARY

> A **synonym** has a similar meaning to another word.
>
> jump   hop

large	cap	hot	glad	jump

Read each sentence. Replace the underlined word with one from the box.

1. I wore a <u>hat</u> to the game.   cap

2. In July, it is often <u>warm</u>.   hot

3. The rabbit will <u>hop</u> over to me.   jump

4. The student was <u>happy</u> it was recess.   glad

5. A <u>big</u> bully was mean to the girl.   large

▶ Contractions

Rule	Example
▶ A **contraction** is one word made of two words put together. One or more letters are left out. An apostrophe (') takes the place of the missing letter or letters.	▶ are not = aren't ▶ did not = didn't
▶ Contractions can be made with the word *not*.	
▶ Contractions can be made with a pronoun and a verb.	▶ I am = I'm ▶ I will = I'll

GRAMMAR AND USAGE

Practice Draw a line to match each pair of words with the correct contraction.

1. I will   we'll

2. we will   they're

3. do not   aren't

4. they are   I'll

5. are not   don't

▶Rhyme

WRITER'S CRAFT

> ▶ Poetry joins the sounds and meanings of words to create ideas and feelings.
>
> ▶ Words that **rhyme** sound alike.

Practice Write two sentences using two rhyming words from the box. The first one has been done for you.

fat	rat	bee	knee	rain	train

1. We were on the train.

2. When it began to rain.

Answers may vary. _____

_____

_____

►Classifying and Categorizing

COMPREHENSION

Focus Readers classify and categorize to help keep track of information that they read.

Here is how to classify and categorize.

► Name the categories, or the **kinds** of things, characters, or events.

For example: **Things That Have Wheels**

Things That Fly

► List the things, characters, or events that fit under each category.

Things That Have Wheels

bike, tricycle, airplane, lawnmower

Things That Fly

airplane, helicopter, hot air balloon

► Sometimes, things, characters, or events can fit into more than one category. For example, *airplane* fits under both **Things That Have Wheels** and **Things That Fly**.

Practice Circle the thing that does not fit in each category.

1. Things to eat with

fork   plate   (slippers)   knife

▶**Classifying and Categorizing**

COMPREHENSION

2. Things to read

books   magazines   map   (pillow)

3. Things to listen to

radio   telephone   (pie)   television

4. Things to cut with

(comb)   lawnmower   knife   scissors

 **Apply** Look at the items in the box. Think of two categories to classify the items into. Write the categories. Then, put the items into the correct category.

| lemonade | strawberries | coffee | milk |
| bananas | orange juice | grapes | watermelon |

Answers may vary. Possible answers are shown.

Category: __Drinks__   Category: __Fruits__

____lemonade____   ____bananas____

____orange juice____   ____strawberries____

____coffee____   ____grapes____

____milk____   ____watermelon____

▶The /ar/ Sound

Say the words *bark* and *harp*. These words have the /ar/ sound spelled *ar*.

farm	yard	part	smart	shark

 Consonant Substitution Strategy
Replace the underlined letter or letters to make a new word. The /ar/ sound will be spelled the same.

1. <u>c</u>art + p = _**part**_

2. <u>ha</u>rd + y = _**yard**_

3. <u>ha</u>rm + f = _**farm**_

4. <u>p</u>art + sm = _**smart**_

5. <u>m</u>ark + sh = _**shark**_

SPELLING

▶ Science Words

Scientists use **science words** to help them explain what they study.

geo means "earth"

bio means "life"

zoo means "animals"

-logist means "someone who studies"

Fill in the blank with what each scientist studies.

1. A <u>geo</u>logist studies the <u>earth</u> .

2. A <u>bio</u>logist studies <u>life</u> .

3. A <u>zoo</u>logist studies <u>animals</u> .

Name _____ Date _____

▶ Linking and Helping Verb Tenses

The **tense** of a verb tells *when* something happens.

Rule	**Example**
▶ The **present tense** tells about something that is happening *now*.	▶ The car **is** in the driveway.
	▶ The boys **are** running in the field.
▶ The **past tense** tells about something that already happened.	▶ The car **was** driving down the street.
	▶ The boys **were** running in the field.

Practice The linking or helping verb is underlined in each sentence. Write *past* or *present* on the line.

1. The zebra <u>is</u> eating.   **present** _____

2. The zebra <u>was</u> in the zoo.   **past** _____

3. Polar bears <u>are</u> in Alaska.   **present** _____

4. The polar bears <u>were</u> cold.   **past** _____

5. The baby elephant <u>is</u> small.   **present** _____

6. The horses <u>were</u> running wild.   **past** _____

▶ Figurative Language

WRITER'S CRAFT

Figures of Speech

▶ A **simile** compares two unlike things by using the word *like* or *as*.

▶ A **metaphor** compares two unlike things without using the word *like* or *as*.

▶ **Personification** gives an object human qualities.

Practice Read each sentence. Circle the two things being compared.

1. Her (hair) was as white as (snow).

2. His (arm) was like (steel).

3. (Kerry) swam like a (fish).

4. Your (hands) are like (ice).

5. His (eyes) are as blue as the (ocean).

Figurative Language • Reteach

▶The /er/ and /or/ Sounds

Say the word *fort*. This word has the /or/ sound spelled *or*.
Say the words *herd*, *swirl*, and *burn*. These words have
the /er/ sound spelled *er*, *ir*, or *ur*.

more	girl	hurt	first	for

Visualization Strategy
Circle the word that is spelled correctly.
Then write the word.

1. hert (hurt) hurt _____

2. (girl) gurl girl _____

3. ferst (first) first _____

4. (for) fer for _____

5. mir (more) more _____

SPELLING

▶ Antonyms

VOCABULARY

> **Antonyms** are opposites.
>
> up   down

Circle the antonym of the underlined word.

1. My shoes are <u>wet</u>.

   (dry)   dirty

2. Gym class is too <u>short</u>.

   (long)   silly

3. The answer is <u>yes</u>.

   four   (no)

4. We turned the light <u>on</u>.

   (off)   behind

5. It is bright <u>outside</u>.

   (inside)   sunny

UNIT 4 Fossils • **Lesson 4** *Why Did the Dinosaurs Disappear?*

▶Nouns: Singular and Plural

GRAMMAR AND USAGE

Rule

▶ Most nouns can be made **plural** by adding *–s* to the end of the word.

▶Nouns that end in *s, x, z, ss, ch,* or *sh* are made plural by adding *–es*.

Rule

▶ Nouns that end with a *consonant* and a *y* are made plural by changing the *y* to an *i* and adding *–es*.

▶ When a noun ends with a *vowel* and a *y*, an *s* is added.

Practice Look at the singular and plural nouns below. Underline the correct spelling for each plural noun.

Singular	Plural	
1. family	familys	<u>families</u>
2. play	<u>plays</u>	plaies
3. box	boxs	<u>boxes</u>
4. dress	dresss	<u>dresses</u>
5. table	<u>tables</u>	tablies
6. lunch	lunchs	<u>lunches</u>

▶ Organizing Descriptive Writing

WRITER'S CRAFT

> ▶ **Descriptions** are words that make a picture in the reader's mind.
>
> ▶ Start your descriptive paragraph with your topic.
>
> ▶ Add details that make a picture in the reader's mind.
>
> ▶ Sum up your main points at the end.

Practice Write a paragraph about your favorite animal or food. Use the describing words in the box to help you.

brown	loud	furry	salty	smooth
soft	round	sweet	blue	prickly

Answers will vary.

_____

_____

_____

_____

_____

_____

▶Collecting and Organizing Data

> ▶Places to find data: **atlas, dictionary, encyclopedia, magazines, newspapers,** and a **museum** or **zoo.**
>
> ▶Ways to organize data: **chart** or **timeline.**

Practice **Tell where you would find and how you would organize data about these topics.**

1. The Solar System ___encyclopedia or museum; chart___

2. Events of the past year ___newspaper or magazine; timeline___

3. Volcanoes ___encyclopedia; chart___

4. Cities in China ___atlas; chart___

5. Where monkeys live ___encyclopedia; chart___

6. Words that begin with "T" ___dictionary; chart___

7. How long dinosaurs lived ___museum or encyclopedia; timeline___

WRITER'S CRAFT

▶ Sequence

Focus Sequence is the order that things happen in a story. A writer uses words called time and order words to help readers follow the sequence of things that happen in a story.

▶ **Order words** show the order that events happen. Words such as *first*, *then*, *next*, and *finally* show order.

▶ **Time words** show how time passes in a story. Words such as *spring*, *tomorrow*, and *morning* show time.

COMPREHENSION

Practice

▶ Look at the pictures. Put the pictures in the right sequence by writing the correct order word on the line below each picture. Use the order words *first*, *then*, and *finally*.

then
_____

first
_____

finally
_____

UNIT 4   Fossils • **Lesson 5** *Monster Tracks*

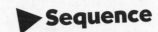

▶**Sequence**

▶**Look at the following sentences about the project in "Monster Tracks." Put the steps in the right sequence by writing the correct order word in the blank. Use the order words *first*, *next*, and *finally*.**

Answers will vary.

1. __next___ Pack wet sand into a box.

2. __finally__ Press the objects into the sand.

3. __first___ Gather some feathers, twigs, bones, seashells, stones, or small sharp rocks.

 **Write a first sentence for the following sequence. Use an order word in your sentence.**

Answers will vary.
Possible answer is shown.

First, I will buy my friend a birthday present.

Next, I will wrap the present.

Finally, I will dress for the birthday party.

COMPREHENSION

UNIT 4 Fossils • **Lesson 5** *Monster Tracks*

▶ Words with *br* and *fr*

SPELLING

Say the words *bright* and *fright*. The letters at the beginning of these words combine to make one sound.

| free | brick | frog | brag | brush |

Pronunciation Strategy
Say each word. Write the words from the box that begin with the same sound.

Order of answers will vary.

bright

1. brick _____

2. brag _____

3. brush _____

fright

4. frog _____

5. free _____

Words with br *and* fr • **Reteach**

▶ Analogies

> **Analogies** compare.
>
> *Peels* are to *bananas* as *rinds* are to *oranges*.

| bed | circle | birds | moon | read |

Complete each analogy with a word from the box.

1. Rabbits are to burrows as

   birds are to nests.

2. Sun is to sunlight as

   moon is to moonlight.

3. Curtain is to window as

   blanket is to **bed**.

4. Cracker is to square as

   pizza is to **circle**.

5. Music is to listen as

   book is to **read**.

VOCABULARY

Name _____ Date _____

▶Adverbs

GRAMMAR AND USAGE

Rule	Example
▶ An **adverb** describes a verb. Adverbs can tell *when, where,* or *how.* Adverbs often end in *-ly,* but not always.	▶ The car was moving **slowly.** (how?) ▶ The dog ran **away.** (where?) ▶ I will return **soon.** (when?)

Practice

▶ Read each sentence. Underline the adverb.

1. I got to school <u>early</u>.

2. The dog ran <u>slowly</u>.

3. The car drove <u>fast</u>.

4. Monika hit the ball <u>hard</u>.

▶ Complete each sentence with an adverb that answers the questions.

Answers will vary. Possible answers are shown.

5. When? Meet me __today__.

6. How? Althea swam __quickly__.

Adverbs • Reteach

▶ Paragraph Form

Make sure your paragraphs:

- ▸ begin on a new line.
- ▸ are indented.
- ▸ have a topic sentence.
- ▸ have supporting details.

   Write a short paragraph about your favorite TV show. Make sure you include all the parts of a paragraph.

Answers will vary. _____

_____

_____

_____

_____

WRITER'S CRAFT

▶Review

SPELLING

white	bring	chase	fish	third

Consonant-Substitution
Replace the underlined letter or letters to create a new word.

1. <u>f</u>ind   +   sh   =   <u>fish</u>

2. <u>b</u>ird   +   th   =   <u>third</u>

3. <u>b</u>ase   +   ch   =   <u>chase</u>

4. <u>k</u>ite   +   wh   =   <u>white</u>

5. <u>s</u>ing   +   br   =   <u>bring</u>

▶Review

> **Synonyms** are similar.
> **Antonyms** are opposites.

Write a synonym and antonym for each word.

Answers will vary.

smile

1. _____

2. _____

great

3. _____

4. _____

angry

5. _____

6. _____

bad

7. _____

8. _____

VOCABULARY

UNIT 4 Fossils • **Lesson 6** *Let's Go Dinosaur Tracking!*

▶Review

GRAMMAR AND USAGE

┌───┐

Rule

▶An **adjective** describes or tells more about a noun or pronoun.

▶An **adverb** is a word that describes a verb.

▶A **contraction** is formed with an apostrophe.

Rule

▶The **present tense** of a verb tells about something that is happening *now*.

▶The **past tense** of a verb tells about something that already happened.

▶A **plural noun** is a word that names more than one person, place, or thing.

└───┘

Practice

▶**Underline the adjectives and circle the adverbs. Add apostrophes to any contractions.**

1. We'll go (quickly) to the <u>new</u> store.

▶**Change the singular noun to a plural noun.**

2. butterfly   <u>**butterflies**</u>

▶**Rewrite the following sentence changing it from past to present tense.**

3. Becca was at the library. <u>**Becca is at the library.**</u>

▶ Topic Sentences

A topic sentence tells what a paragraph is about. You can tell your topic in the first sentence of a paragraph.

Example

Playing soccer is fun. You get to meet new friends. You are part of a team. It's fun to kick the ball.

 **Write a topic sentence that goes with these details.**

Poems are easy to write.

_____

_____

All you need are thoughts and ideas.

Write your ideas on paper.

Then, put your ideas into verses.

Read your poem and make changes if you want.

Read your poem to a friend.

WRITER'S CRAFT

▶ Point of View

Focus Point of view is how the author decides to tell the story.

First-person point of view is when

▶ The storyteller is a character in the story.

▶ The clue words *I, me, my, we, us,* and *our* are used.
   I wish I could go too.

Third-person point of view is when

▶ The storyteller is not a character in the story.

▶ The clue words *she, her, hers, he, him, his, they,* and *theirs* are used.
   She can stand on her head.

Practice Tell whether the following sentences are first-person point of view or third-person point of view. Underline the clue words that helped you decide.

1. <u>I</u> never walk to school alone. <u>I</u> always walk with <u>my</u> best friend, Jim.

   first-person point of view
   _____

2. Roberta was the fastest runner in our school. But <u>I</u> had been practicing all summer. Now <u>I</u> was very fast, too.

   first-person point of view
   _____

COMPREHENSION

▶**Point of View**

3. Terry's shirt was a little dirty from playing outside. So <u>he</u> put on a clean one before dinner.

<u>**third-person point of view**</u>

4. Martha did not like pears. Whenever <u>she</u> saw them <u>she</u> said, "Eww."

<u>**third-person point of view**</u>

 **Read each sentence below. Decide if it is first-person point of view or third-person point of view. Write a *1* on the line for first-person, or write a *3* for third-person. Remember to look for the clue words to help you decide.**

1. _**1**_ I asked my brother for the video game.

2. _**3**_ Dina saw him wave to her.

3. _**3**_ Sam asked if he could go too.

4. _**3**_ They had a good time at the party.

5. _**1**_ We can't wait for our vacation in New York City.

COMPREHENSION

UNIT 5 Courage • **Lesson I** *Molly the Brave and Me*

►Words Ending in *-ed* and *-ing*

slip + ed = slipped

slip + ing = slipping

Many one syllable words with short-vowel sounds add an additional letter before an ending is added.

| **hitting** | **missed** | **hopped** | **slipped** | **skipping** |

Rhyming Strategy
Write a word from the box that rhymes with each word below. Notice the double-consonant in each word.

1. mo<u>pp</u>ed   hopped _____

2. ri<u>pp</u>ing   skipping _____

3. si<u>tt</u>ing   hitting _____

4. ki<u>ss</u>ed   missed _____

5. fli<u>pp</u>ed   slipped _____

SPELLING

▶Synonyms

A **synonym** has a similar meaning to another word.

small   tiny

| nice   thin   sad   bright   tall |

Read each sentence. Which word from the box can replace the underlined word?

1. The little boy was <u>blue</u> and unhappy. <u>sad</u>

2. She learned to write with a <u>skinny</u> pencil. <u>thin</u>

3. My teacher is very <u>kind</u>. <u>nice</u>

4. The building was very <u>high</u>. <u>tall</u>

5. My scooter is very <u>shiny</u>. <u>bright</u>

VOCABULARY

MECHANICS

▶Capitalization: *I* and Proper Nouns

Rule	**Example**
▶The word *I* is *always* written with a capital letter.	▶Michelle and **I** are late for school.
▶A **proper noun** is a special type of a noun. Proper nouns begin with a capital letter. A proper noun names a *particular* person, place, or thing.	▶**K**yle and **S**eth ▶**R**ichmond, **V**irginia ▶**L**ake **E**rie ▶**U**nited **S**tates

Practice

▶**Underline the proper nouns in each sentence.**

1. Lewis Carroll wrote a great book.

2. Alicia went to the Olympics in Los Angeles, California.

3. Mark went to the San Diego Zoo with Hillary and Oscar.

▶**Complete each sentence using a proper noun.**

4. Richard has a sister named _____ **Answers will vary.** _____.

5. Rachael went on vacation to _____.

Capitalization: I and Proper Nouns • Reteach

Name _____ Date _____

▶Organizing Narrative Writing

▶**Narrative writing** tells a story.

   Your narrative paragraph should have:

▶A topic

▶Details that go with the topic.

▶A closing sentence

Be sure to tell what the story is about, who is in the story, and where it takes place.

Practice Write a paragraph telling about something you did last summer. It could be a trip you took, a sport you played, or a new friend you met.

Answers will vary.

_____

_____

_____

_____

UNIT 5 **Courage • Lesson 2** *Dragons and Giants*

▶ Present Tense of Words

SPELLING

> Today, I will _____.
> Words that fit in this sentence are in the present tense.

sing	drive	give	tell	look

 Consonant-Substitution Strategy Change the underlined letter or letters to spell a new word. Then write and read the word in the sentence.

1. <u>t</u>ook + l = **look**

Today, I will **look** .

2. <u>d</u>ing + s = **sing**

Today, I will **sing** .

3. <u>d</u>ive + dr = **drive**

Today, I will **drive** .

4. <u>l</u>ive + g = **give**

Today, I will **give** .

5. <u>sp</u>ell + t = **tell**

Today, I will **tell** .

Name _____ Date _____

▶Antonyms

> **Antonyms** are opposites.
>
> cold   hot

day	light	full	over	out

Write a word from the box next to its antonym.

1. dark __light_____

2. under __over_____

3. empty __full_____

4. night __day_____

5. in __out_____

UNIT 5 Courage • **Lesson 2** *Dragons and Giants*

▶Conjunctions and Interjections

Rule	**Example**
▶**Conjunctions** connect words or groups of words in a sentence. Some conjunctions: *and, but, or.*	▶Jerry **and** Phil will play Tuesday **or** Wednesday. ▶I would go, **but** I have baseball practice.
▶An **interjection** is a word that shows strong feeling or emotions. An interjection is followed by an exclamation point (**!**).	▶**Wow!** I got an A+ on the test. ▶**Great!** You must be smart.

Practice

▶**Circle the conjunctions in the sentences below.**

1. The Rocky Mountains are in Colorado (and) Idaho.

2. Mountains are made of peaks (and) valleys.

▶**Circle the interjections in the sentences below.**

3. "(Wow!) The highest point is over 14,000 feet high," said Dolores.

4. "(Oh boy!) I wouldn't want to climb that," said Stacey.

UNIT 5 Courage • **Lesson 2** *Dragons and Giants*

▶Plot

> The **plot** of a story:
> ▶ Has characters, a setting, and a problem to solve.

Practice Write ideas for possible plots based on the information below.

1. **Setting:** a bakery

   Characters: baker, owner, and worker

   Answers will vary. _____

   _____

2. **Setting:** the woods

   Characters: two boys, a dog, and a bear

   Answers will vary. _____

   _____

3. **Setting:** a party

   Characters: a group of kids, parents

   Answers will vary. _____

   _____

▶ Suspense and Surprise

> ▶ **Suspense** makes the reader want to find out what happens next.
>
> ▶ **Surprise** is when something happens that the reader didn't expect.

Practice   **Read each paragraph. Circle the letter of the paragraph that has a surprise ending.**

Ⓐ The deep-sea diver climbed back in the boat. She was more excited than she could remember. What a find! In an unexplored old wreck, she found an odd-shaped bottle. She took the cork out of the bottle. A huge cloud of smoke burst from it. When the smoke cleared, there stood . . . a puppy!

B. The deep-sea diver climbed back in the boat. She was more excited than she could remember. What a find! In an unexplored old wreck, she found a beautiful, odd-shaped bottle. She took the cork out of the bottle. A huge cloud of smoke burst from it. When the smoke cleared, there stood a genie!

▶ Cause and Effect

Focus Seeing cause and effect relationships between the events in a story will help a reader understand the story better.

> A **cause** is *why* something happens.
>
> An **effect** is *what* happens.
>
> > Because some animals blend into their surroundings, ⟵ **Cause**
> >
> > they are hard to see. ⟵ **Effect**

Practice For each sentence below, circle the cause and underline the effect.

1. I visited the doctor because (I had a sore throat.)

2. (Everyone was in the car,) so we were ready to go.

3. The dog started barking because (he heard a noise.)

4. (I don't like pink lemonade,) so I drank water.

5. Marvin went back inside because (he forgot his lunch.)

6. (Catherine couldn't keep her eyes open,) so she went to bed.

7. My dad drove me to school because (I missed the bus.)

8. (The store was closed,) so we had to go to another store.

COMPREHENSION

UNIT 5 Courage • **Lesson 3** *The Hole in the Dike*

▶ **Cause and Effect**

Read each sentence. Write the effect and the cause. The first one is done for you.

9. I wore my jacket because it was chilly outside.

Effect: I wore my jacket. _____

Cause: It was chilly outside. _____

10. Because it was his birthday, we baked a cake.

Effect: **We baked a cake.** _____

Cause: **It was his birthday.** _____

11. The deer hid when he smelled the hunters.

Effect: **The deer hid.** _____

Cause: **He smelled the hunters.** _____

12. It's hot today, so we're going for a swim.

Effect: **We're going for a swim.** _____

Cause: **It's hot today.** _____

 **Finish the sentence below. Add an effect.**

Answers will vary.

Jackie wanted to play baseball _____

_____

COMPREHENSION

UNIT 5 Courage • **Lesson 3** *The Hole in the Dike*

▶Past Tense of Words

Yesterday, I _____.
Words that fit in this sentence are in the past tense.

| sang | drove | slid | told | looked |

Consonant-Substitution Strategy
Change the underlined letter or letters to spell a new word. Then write and read the word in the sentence.

1. rang + s = **sang**

Yesterday, I **sang** _____.

2. dove + dr = **drove**

Yesterday, I **drove** _____.

3. hid + sl = **slid**

Yesterday, I **slid** _____.

4. sold + t = **told**

Yesterday, I **told** _____.

5. cooked + l = **looked**

Yesterday, I **looked** _____.

UNIT 5 Courage • **Lesson 3** *The Hole in the Dike*

► Base Word Families

A **base word** is a word that can stand alone.

It gives you a clue to the meaning of other words in its family.

Base Word	**Base Word Family Members**
bird	birdbath
	songbird

Underline the base word in each pair of words. Then make a new base word family word. The first one is done for you.

1. <u>eat</u>en   <u>eat</u>ing

   eat   + s   = **eats** _____

2. <u>slow</u>ing   <u>slow</u>est

   slow + er = **slower** _____

3. <u>win</u>ner   <u>win</u>s

   win   + ing = **winning** _____

4. <u>eye</u>lash   <u>eye</u>brow

   eye   + lid = **eyelid** _____

VOCABULARY

▶Commas in Dialogue

Rule	**Example**
▶ A **comma** (,) separates the quotation marks from the rest of the sentence.	▶"Let's go camping," *said LaShauna.* ▶Jessica asked, "Where should we go camping?" ▶"In the woods," answered Rebecca.

MECHANICS

Practice

▶**Put commas where they belong in each sentence.**

1. "My rabbit eats lettuce," said Vicki.

2. Wilbur asked, "Does he like carrots?"

3. "Yes, he does," answered Vicki.

▶**Put commas where they belong in each sentence. Put an X though any commas used incorrectly.**

4. "My rabbit's name is Gregory," said Sarah.

5. Alyssa asked, "Do rabbits make good pets?"

▶Characterization

Writers tell what characters do, say, think, and feel by using **Characterization.**

WRITER'S CRAFT

Practice **Write a sentence that tells what each person might do, say, think, or feel.**

1. Write what your parent might do at a play.

Answers will vary.

_____

2. Write what your friend might say at a party.

Answers will vary.

_____

3. Write what your teacher might think at lunch.

Answers will vary.

_____

4. Write how you might feel on a holiday.

Answers will vary.

_____

▶Setting

The **setting** of a story is the time and place in which the story happens.

Practice Read each paragraph. Underline the words that tell when the story happens. Circle the words that tell where the story takes place.

1. July has never been this hot. The summer sun baked the earth. The green fields of corn turned brown.

2. A hush fell over the dark city. Snowflakes as big as quarters fell from the night sky. Snow covered the city streets.

3. As I lay on my blanket in the sand, I could hear the waves breaking on the shore. I closed my eyes and felt the afternoon sun on my face.

WRITER'S CRAFT

▶Plurals

Words ending in **-s** and **-es** often mean "more than one." **Plural** is another word for "more than one." The words *foxes* and *cats* are plural words.

ducks	stores	glasses	buses	wishes

Vowel-Substitution Strategy
Change the underlined letter or letters to spell a new word. Underline the letter or letters that make the word plural.

1. gl<u>o</u>sses + a = <u>glass<u>es</u></u>

2. b<u>a</u>ses + u = <u>bus<u>es</u></u>

3. d<u>e</u>cks + u = <u>duck<u>s</u></u>

4. w<u>a</u>shes + i = <u>wish<u>es</u></u>

5. st<u>a</u>res + o = <u>stor<u>es</u></u>

▶Prefixes

A **prefix** is added to the beginning of a word.

The prefix *pre-* can change a word to mean "before."

pre + game = "before game"

A singer sang at the <u>pregame</u> show.

▶ **Add the prefix *pre-*, then write what the word means.**

1. pre + dawn = _**predawn**_____

meaning: _**before dawn**_____

2. pre + test = _**pretest**_____

meaning: _**before test**_____

The prefix *re-* can change a word to mean "again."

re + tie = "tie again"

He had to stop running and <u>retie</u> his shoe.

▶ **Add the prefix *re-*, then write what the word means.**

3. re + try = _**retry**_____

meaning: _**try again**_____

4. re + read = _**reread**_____

meaning: _**read again**_____

VOCABULARY

▶Capitalization: Titles and Initials

MECHANICS

Rule	Example
▶A person's name is always capitalized. A **title,** which comes before a person's name, is also capitalized.	▶**Mrs.** Lopez spoke to the class today.
	▶**Dr.** Wilson drove to the hospital.
	▶**General** Washington commanded the troops.
▶**Initials** of a person's name are also capitalized.	▶**E.B.** White wrote <u>Charlotte's Web</u>.

Practice Rewrite the following names using the correct capitalization.

1. c.s. Lewis ___C.S. Lewis_____

2. sergeant harris ___Sergeant Harris_____

3. mrs. Wilcox ___Mrs. Wilcox_____

4. a.j. Anderson ___A.J. Anderson_____

5. p.j. O'Connor ___P.J. O'Connor_____

▶Dialogue

Dialogue tells the reader exactly what the characters say.

Remember to:

▶ Put quotation marks (" ") before and after a speaker's exact words.

Practice **Read each sentence. Add quotation marks where they are needed.**

1. "What did Joe say?"asked Marty.

2. "Linda asked if she could go,"said Mom.

3. "Hurry up,"Bruce shouted. "We'll be late!"

4. "Can we go now?"asked Tracie.

WRITER'S CRAFT

COMPREHENSION

▶ Sequence

Focus Knowing when things happen in a story and the order in which things happen can help you understand the story.

> **Sequence** means the order in which things happen in a story. Here are examples of time and order words that help show the sequence in a story.
>
> *today, yesterday, once upon a time, first, then, later, finally, next*

Practice Read the sentences. Underline the time and order words in each sentence.

1. <u>Today</u> is my dog's birthday.

2. Did you get the newspaper <u>yesterday</u>?

3. I want to go shopping <u>later</u>.

4. <u>First</u>, let's get an ice cream cone.

5. <u>Then</u>, we are going on a field trip.

6. <u>Finally</u>, I put on my coat.

7. I am going to visit the dentist <u>tomorrow</u>.

8. <u>Next</u>, I put on my shoes.

▶**Sequence**

▶ **Use the words in the box below to complete the sentences.**   **Answers will vary.**

tomorrow	yesterday	today

9. Gretchen is coming __today__ to pick up the cat.

10. The books are due __tomorrow__.

11. It was foggy __yesterday__.

▶ **Number the following sentences in the order in which they happen. Circle the order words.**

12. __3__ (Finally) the show began.

13. __1__ (First,) we found our seats at the circus.

14. __2__ (Next,) we watched the spotlights start to flash.

 **Write a sentence using one of the words below.**

today   yesterday   **Answers will vary.**

_____

_____

COMPREHENSION

UNIT 5 Courage • **Lesson 5** *The Empty Pot*

▶ Suffixes

SPELLING

> high + er = higher
>
> silly + er = sillier
>
> Words ending in *y* may require a spelling change when an ending is added.

sillier	higher	slower	slowest	happiest

Visualization Strategy
Circle the word that is spelled correctly. Then write the word.

1. slowr   (slower)   slower

2. sillyer   (sillier)   sillier

3. (slowest) slowst   slowest

4. highr   (higher)   higher

5. happyest   (happiest)   happiest

▶ Suffixes

A **suffix** is added to the end of a word. The suffix *-er* changes a word so that it means "more."

soft + er = "more soft"

My pillow is <u>softer</u> than my bed.

Add the suffix *-er*, then write what the word means. The first one is done for you.

1. loud + er = louder

   meaning: more loud

2. cold + er = **colder**

   meaning: **more cold**

3. slow + er = **slower**

   meaning: **more slow**

4. smart + er = **smarter**

   meaning: **more smart**

5. green + er = **greener**

   meaning: **more green**

VOCABULARY

▶ Apostrophes and Colons

MECHANICS

Rule	Example
▶ An **apostrophe (')** is used in **contractions** and **possessives**.	▶ **She's** She is ▶ Martha's car is red.
▶ A **colon (:)** is used before a list of items or a series.	▶ Please buy these items at the store: milk, bread, lettuce, ketchup, and cheese.
▶ A colon is also used when writing the time. It is placed between the hour and the minutes.	▶ The alarm will ring at 7:15.

Practice   Read the following sentences. Add apostrophes and colons where they belong.

1. John's recital starts at 4:00.

2. Things to remember: John's violin, his bow, and his carrying case.

3. John's teacher wants him to be at the recital by 3:15.

▶Sentence Combining

> ▶ Two sentences with ideas that are alike can be put together, or combined by using the word *and*.
>
> ▶ Remember to put a comma before the word *and* when combining sentences.

Practice **Combine the following sentence pairs.**

1. The snow fell quickly. It was beautiful.

The snow fell quickly, and it was beautiful.

2. It was late. Sammy had to go.

It was late, and Sammy had to go.

3. Practice was over. Lin saw his mom.

Practice was over, and Lin saw his mom.

4. The bee flew. It buzzed in my ear.

The bee flew, and it buzzed in my ear.

5. The bell rang. The teacher stopped talking.

The bell rang, and the teacher stopped talking.

WRITER'S CRAFT

▶ Author's Purpose

Focus **Writers have different reasons for writing.**

Writers write to inform.

- ▶ Includes facts
- ▶ Includes information that can be proven

Writers write to entertain.

- ▶ Includes funny words or events
- ▶ Includes exciting or familiar events

Writers write to persuade.

- ▶ Includes opinions
- ▶ May include facts to support opinions

Writers write to explain how.

- ▶ Includes directions
- ▶ Shows steps and sequence

Practice **Read each group of sentences. Tell if they were written to *entertain* or to *inform*.**

1. There are nine planets. The one farthest from Earth is called Pluto.

   These sentences were written to ___inform___.

Author's Purpose • Reteach

COMPREHENSION

▶ **Author's Purpose**

2. Robbie didn't know what to do when the cow said to him, "Why don't you have a glass of milk? It will make you feel better."

These sentences were written to __entertain_____.

 **Apply** **In the box are purposes for writing. Read each story title, then choose the best purpose for each story. Write the purpose on the line.**

inform	entertain	persuade	explain how

1. How to Make Spaghetti

__explain how_____

2. Facts About Fish

__inform_____

3. Frogs Are Better Pets Than Snakes

__persuade_____

4. The Great Snake Escape

__entertain_____

5. How to Make a Peanut Butter and Jelly Sandwich

__explain how_____

COMPREHENSION

▶Review

SPELLING

animals	trapped	aunts	packed	uncles

 Conventions Strategy
Add the endings to create a new word.

1. aunt   +   s   =   **aunts**

2. uncle   +   s   =   **uncles**

3. trap   +   ed   =   **trapped**

4. animal   +   s   =   **animals**

5. pack   +   ed   =   **packed**

Which words in the box are plurals?

Order of answers may vary

6. **aunts**

7. **uncles**

8. **animals**

UNIT 5 Courage • **Lesson 6** *Brave as a Mountain Lion*

▶Prefixes

A **prefix** is added to the beginning of a word.

The prefix *mis-* can change a word to mean "wrong."

    mis + dial = "dial wrong"

Don't <u>misdial</u> the number because you are in a hurry.

VOCABULARY

▶**Add the prefix *mis-*, then write what the word means.**

1. mis   +   use   =   <u>misuse</u>

    meaning: <u>use wrong</u>

2. mis   +   cut   =   <u>miscut</u>

    meaning: <u>cut wrong</u>

The prefix *dis-* can change a word to mean "not."

    dis + obey = "not obey"

It is rude to <u>disobey</u> your teacher.

▶**Add the prefix *dis-*, then write what the word means.**

3. dis   +   like   =   <u>dislike</u>

    meaning: <u>not like</u>

4. dis   +   trust   =   <u>distrust</u>

    meaning: <u>not trust</u>

▶ Review

GRAMMAR AND USAGE

<table>
<tr><td>

Rule

▶ The word *I*, proper nouns, titles, and initials in a name are always **capitalized**.

▶ **Conjunctions** connect words or groups of words in a sentence.

▶ An **interjection** is a word that shows strong feeling or emotions.

</td><td>

Rule

▶ A **comma (,)** separates the quotation marks from the rest of the sentence.

▶ An **apostrophe (')** is used in **contractions**.

▶ A **colon (:)** is used to introduce a list of items, and is used in writing time.

</td></tr>
</table>

Practice Read the following sentences. Add the correct punctuation. Underline words that should be capitalized.

1. Oh, my! We need to leave now to get to centerville by 9:45.

2. d.j. Cranston said, "i'm eating dinner with doctor rafique at sullivan's steakhouse restaurant."

3. The ingredients are: salt, pepper, water, and potatoes.

▶ Time and Order Words

Some words tell when something happens. Other words tell the order in which things happen.

Here are some time and order words.

Time Words	Order Words
today	first
yesterday	next
next week	finally

Practice Read each sentence. Underline the time and order words. Then write *T* if it is a time word or *O* if it is an order word.

1. <u>Last week</u>, we went to our school's band concert. ___**T**___

2. <u>First</u>, we heard the violins. ___**O**___

3. <u>Then</u>, the trumpets joined in. ___**O**___

4. <u>Next</u> came the drums. ___**O**___

5. <u>Later</u>, there was a flute solo. ___**T**___

6. <u>Next year</u>, I want to play in the band. ___**T**___

WRITER'S CRAFT

▶ Prefixes

> <u>un</u>pack
>
> <u>re</u>pack
>
> The prefixes *re-* and *un-* are added to the beginning of words.

retake	unsure	unlock	retry

 Visualization Strategy
Write a word from the box that rhymes with each word below. Underline the prefix.

1. refry   <u>re</u>try

2. unpure   <u>un</u>sure

3. remake   <u>re</u>take

4. unblock   <u>un</u>lock

▶ Social Studies Words

VOCABULARY

> **Social studies words** help us compare other cultures to our own.

igloos	traded	hunted

Write the word from the box that completes the sentence.

1. We may live in a house, but some people in very cold

   places live in __igloos__.

2. We buy food at the store, but the first Americans __hunted__ for food.

3. We pay money for food, while some people __traded__ other goods for food.

▶Review

Rule

▶A noun is a person, place, or thing. A **proper noun** is capitalized. A **common noun** is *not* capitalized.

▶**Subject pronouns** are I, you, he, she, it, we, you, they.

▶**Object pronouns** are me, you, him, her, it, us, you, them.

Rule

▶An **action verb** tells what someone is doing.

▶A **possessive noun** ends in apostrophe s (**'s**) or just an apostrophe (**'**).

▶A **possessive pronoun** takes the place of a possessive noun.

Practice

▶**Read the sentence. Circle the common nouns and underline the proper nouns.**

1. <u>Mount Rainier</u> is the highest (mountain) in <u>Washington</u>.

▶**Read the sentence. Circle the subject pronouns and underline the object pronouns.**

2. (She) gave a present to <u>him</u>.

▶**Write the correct possessive of the noun.**

3. teacher <u>teacher's</u>

Name _____ Date _____

▶ Audience and Purpose

Your **audience** is the person or people who will read your writing.

Your **purpose** is your reason for writing. There are four main purposes for writing.

▶ To **inform**   To **entertain**

▶ To **explain**   To **persuade**

Practice **For each type of writing, tell what the audience and purpose might be.**

1. A book report __inform; your teacher, classmates__

2. A birthday card __entertain; your friend, a family member__

3. A poster telling about puppies for sale __persuade; dog lovers; children__

4. Directions on how to play a board game __explain; your family, friends, game-lovers__

5. A joke book __entertain; your friends, people who like jokes__

WRITER'S CRAFT

▶ Cause and Effect

COMPREHENSION

Focus Looking for causes and effects helps you better understand story events.

- A **cause** is why something happens.

- An **effect** is what happens as a result.

Practice

▶ **Read each sentence below. Then, answer the questions. The first one is done for you.**

1. My boot was wet because I stepped in a puddle.

   What happened? <u>My boot was wet</u>

   Why did it happen? <u>I stepped in a puddle</u>

2. Courtney did well on the test because she studied.

   What happened? <u>Courtney did well on her test</u>

   Why did it happen? <u>She studied</u>

3. I laughed at the clown's magic trick.

   What happened? <u>I laughed</u>

   Why did it happen? <u>The clown's magic trick</u>

UNIT 6 Our Country and Its People • **Lesson 2** *New Hope*

▶**Cause and Effect**

▶**Write the effect (what happened) and the cause (why the effect happened) in each sentence below.**

4. I visited my grandmother because it was her birthday.

Effect: **I visited my grandmother** _____

Cause: **It was her birthday** _____

5. The game was cancelled because of the bad weather.

Effect: **The game was cancelled** _____

Cause: **The bad weather** _____

6. I drank a glass of water because I was thirsty.

Effect: **I drank a glass of water** _____

Cause: **I was thirsty** _____

7. The flowers we planted last spring were pretty, so we planted them again.

Effect: **We planted them again** _____

Cause: **The flowers we planted last spring were pretty** _____

 **Write a cause-and-effect sentence about losing your favorite toy. Answers will vary.**

_____

_____

COMPREHENSION

▶ Suffixes

SPELLING

help<u>ful</u>
help<u>less</u>

The suffixes **-ful** and **-less** are added to the end of words.

| hopeful | useless | shameless | harmful | helpless |

Consonant-Substitution Strategy
Replace the underlined suffix to create a new word.

1. use<u>ful</u>   +   less   =   __useless__

2. hope<u>less</u>   +   ful   =   __hopeful__

3. help<u>ful</u>   +   less   =   __helpless__

4. harm<u>less</u>   +   ful   =   __harmful__

5. shame<u>less</u> +   ful   =   __shameful__

▶Suffixes

A **suffix** is added to the end of a word. The suffix *-ful* may change a word so that it means "full of" or "having."

color + ful = "full of color"

The box contained 64 <u>colorful</u> crayons.

VOCABULARY

▶**Draw a line from the word with *-ful* added to the words that tell what it means.**

1. careful   having pain

2. fearful   having care

3. painful   having fear

▶**Add the suffix *-ful*, then write what the word means.**

Answers will vary.

4. hurt + ful = <u>**hurtful**</u>

    meaning: <u>**having hurt**</u>

5. pride + ful = <u>**prideful**</u>

    meaning: <u>**having pride**</u>

▶Review

Rule	**Example**
▶The names of **days** and **months** are capitalized.	▶A **comma** is used between the name of a city and state.
▶**Commas** are used in the greeting and closing of a letter.	▶A **comma** is used between the day and the year when writing a date.
▶A **comma** is used after each item in a list.	▶**Quotation marks** are used to show the words of a speaker.
	▶Titles of books and movies are underlined.

Practice Rewrite the sentences using correct punctuation.

1. Tom let Terrell borrow his bike video game and video of

   101 Dalmatians. Tom let Terrell borrow his bike, video

   game, and video of 101 Dalmatians.

2. Marcia said, I want to visit Chicago Illinois, on May 10 2006.

   Marcia said, "I want to visit Chicago, Illinois on May 10,

   2006."

Words of Request

To ask for things in a polite way, use **words of request**.

Words of Request:

Please   Would you

May I   Could you

Practice **Rewrite each sentence using words of request.**

1. Hand me that book.

  Should start with Please, Would you, or Could you.
  _____

2. Call me after school.

  Should start with Please, Would you, or Could you.
  _____

3. I want to go out tonight.

  Should start with May I.
  _____

4. Send me a game that works.

  Should start with Please, Would you, or Could you.
  _____

5. I want to have another piece of cake.

  Should start with May I.
  _____

WRITER'S CRAFT

UNIT 6 Our Country and Its People • **Lesson 3** *A Place Called Freedom*

▶ # Compound Words

A **compound word** is a word made from two words.

rail + road = railroad

| sunrise | maybe | nobody | bedroom | everyone |

Conventions Strategy
Combine the words to create new words.

1. bed   +   room   =   <u>**bedroom**</u>

2. no   +   body   =   <u>**nobody**</u>

3. sun   +   rise   =   <u>**sunrise**</u>

4. may   +   be   =   <u>**maybe**</u>

5. every   +   one   =   <u>**everyone**</u>

Name _____ Date _____

▶Compound Words

> A **compound word** is a word made from two words.
>   sail + boat = sailboat

Read each sentence. Look for words inside the underlined word. Figure out what the hard word means and write it on the line. Answers will vary.

1. I love to spend a day at the <u>seashore</u>.

seashore means: a __**shore**_____ by

the __**sea**_____

2. The <u>sunrise</u> over the water is pretty.

sunrise means: the __**rise**_____ of the __**sun**_____

3. We love to collect <u>seashells</u>.

seashells are: __**shells**_____ from the __**sea**_____

4. Sometimes, there is also <u>seaweed</u> on the shore.

seaweed is: __**weed**_____ from the __**sea**_____

5. Walking on sand in the <u>moonlight</u> is fun.

moonlight means: __**light**_____ from the __**moon**_____

VOCABULARY

Name _____ Date _____

▶Review

GRAMMAR AND USAGE

Complete Sentences

Rule

▶ Complete sentences have a **subject** and a **predicate,** and the subject and verb must agree.

▶ **Run-on sentences** are one sentence that should be two.

Rule

▶ **Sentence fragments** are incomplete sentences because they are missing a subject or predicate.

▶ **Linking verbs** join parts of a sentence to make them complete.

▶ **Helping verbs** tell when something is happening.

Practice

▶ Underline the **subject** and circle the **predicate.**

1. The <u>equator</u> (circles the earth.)

▶ Rewrite the run-on sentence as two sentences. Underline any linking or helping verbs in the new sentences.

2. The oceans are made up of salt water there are four oceans.

The oceans <u>are</u> made up of salt water. There <u>are</u> four

oceans.

UNIT 6 **Our Country and Its People** • **Lesson 3** *A Place Called Freedom*

▶ Structure of Scripts

> ▶ A **script** tells people what to say.
>
> ▶ Scripts also tell people what to do. Stage directions are usually put in ( ) or [ ].

Practice **Write a short script for the following example.**

Example: Vicki and Molly are talking about their favorite movie.

Vicki: **Answers will vary.** _____

Molly: _____

Vicki: _____

Molly: _____

Vicki: _____

Molly: _____

WRITER'S CRAFT

UNIT 6 **Our Country and Its People** • **Lesson 4** *The Story of the Statue of Liberty*

▶ Homophones

> **Homophones** are words that sound alike. They are not spelled the same and do not have the same meaning.

road	meet	two	fourth	piece

 Meaning Strategy
Write the correct homophone in the sentence.

1. One plus __two__ is three.

2. The __fourth__ month is April.

3. A street is a __road__.

4. Where should we __meet__?

5. I want a __piece__ of pie.

SPELLING

▶ Homophones

Homophones are words that sound alike. They are not spelled the same and do not have the same meaning.

Write the word from the box that completes the homophone pair. The first one is done for you.

here	forth	one	dear	red
ewe	way	weak	buy	dough

1. deer   dear

2. week   weak

3. doe   dough

4. hear   here

5. weigh   way

6. read   red

7. fourth   forth

8. won   one

9. you   ewe

10. by   buy

VOCABULARY

GRAMMAR AND USAGE

▶ Adjectives, Adverbs, and Contractions

Rule	**Example**
▶ **Adjectives** describe or tell more about a noun or pronoun.	▶ The desert is **hot** and **dry.**
▶ **Adverbs** describe a verb.	▶ He ran **quickly** to second base.
▶ **Contractions** are formed with an apostrophe.	▶ She will She'll He is He's Does not Doesn't

Practice

▶ **Underline the adjectives and circle the adverbs.**

1. Bill left (early) to go to the <u>surprise</u> party.

2. She is running (around) the <u>large</u> track.

▶ **Rewrite the words as contractions.**

3. can not <u>can't</u>

4. they are <u>they're</u>

▶ Making Inferences

Focus Instead of telling readers everything, writers sometimes just give hints. Readers must use what they already know to understand the story.

> Readers can use what they already know to figure out details that the author left out. Read this sentence.
>
> *Thomas put on his gold crown.*
>
> A reader knows that a king or prince would have a gold crown. So the clue "his gold crown" helps the reader make the inference that Thomas is probably a king or prince.

Practice Read each sentence below. Then write the inference you can make.

1. The wind blew our plates and napkins off the blanket.

   Inference: **It is a windy day. The people are on a picnic.**

   _____

2. When the curtains closed at the end of our performance, everyone clapped.

   Inference: **Everyone enjoyed the performance. The**

   performance was a success.

COMPREHENSION

▶**Making Inferences**

COMPREHENSION

3. John said, "Learning to swim takes a lot of practice."

Inference: **John is learning how to swim. He has spent a lot of time practicing.**

4. Every day, we feed the chickens and milk the cows.

Inference: **The people live on a farm or in the country.**

 **Read the paragraph below. On the lines, write an inference that can be made about what is happening.**

Answers will vary. Possible answer is shown.

The sun disappeared behind the clouds and the sky turned gray. Big drops of rain began to fall. Everyone ran for his or her tent. The rain put out the campfire. The food left out got wet and soggy.

The people are camping when it begins to rain.

▶Homographs

Homographs are words that have the same spelling, but different pronunciations and meanings.

| live | sow | tear | read | wind |

Pronunciation Strategy
Write the homograph that rhymes with both words.

1. bed   need   <u>read</u>

2. find   grinned   <u>wind</u>

3. hive   give   <u>live</u>

4. cow   no   <u>sow</u>

5. pear   fear   <u>tear</u>

SPELLING

▶Homographs

> **Homographs** are words that have the same spelling, but different pronunciations and meanings.
>
> *sow* may mean "female pig" or "plant seed"
>
> *wound* may mean "did wind" or "hurt"

VOCABULARY

Say the homograph and write its meaning.

Answers may vary.

Say *wound* so that it rhymes with *found*.

1. I wound the ball of yarn for the kitty.

   wound means ___did wind___

Say *sow* so that it rhymes with *now*.

2. The sow rolled happily in the mud.

   sow means ___female pig___

Say *sow* so that it rhymes with *blow*.

3. Sunflower seeds are easy to sow and grow.

   sow means ___plant seed___

Name _____ Date _____

▶Review

Rule	Rule
▶ **Linking verbs** join parts of a sentence. ▶ **Helping verbs** are used with action verbs. ▶ The **present tense** of a verb tells about something that is happening *now*.	▶ A **past tense** of a verb tells about something that *already* happened. ▶ **Plural nouns** are more than one person, place, or thing.

Practice

▶ **Circle the present tense verbs and underline the past tense verbs in the sentences below.**

1. February (is) the shortest month.

2. Last year <u>was</u> leap year, and February <u>had</u> 29 days.

▶ **Circle the correct plural for each singular noun.**

Singular	Plural	
3. daisy	(daisies)	daisyes
4. rock	rockes	(rocks)

GRAMMAR AND USAGE

▶Words of Request

WRITER'S CRAFT

> To ask for things in a polite way, use words of request.
> Words of Request:
> Please   Would you
> May I   Could you

Practice   **Rewrite each sentence using words of request.**

1. Bring me more bread.

Should start with Please, Would you, or Could you.
_____

2. I want to go swimming.

Should start with May I.
_____

3. Explain it to me.

Should start with Please, Would you, or Could you.
_____

4. Drive me to Beth's house.

Should start with Please, Would you, or Could you.
_____

5. I want to see that movie.

Should start with May I.
_____

▶ Words with Foreign Origins

> Words from other languages may have different spelling patterns.
>
> pint<u>o</u>
> yod<u>el</u>
> ber<u>et</u>

SPELLING

| nickel | bronco | burro | pretzel | ballet |

Foreign Language Strategy
Write the words that share the underlined spelling patterns.

pint<u>o</u>

1. <u>burro</u>

2. <u>bronco</u>

yod<u>el</u>

3. <u>pretzel</u>

4. <u>nickel</u>

ber<u>et</u>

5. <u>ballet</u>

▶ Multicultural Words

VOCABULARY

> Some words tell us from which culture things come. Something from America is <u>American</u>.

Write the name of the country that completes the sentence.

1. Something from **Brazil** _____ is <u>Brazilian</u>.

2. Something from **India** _____ is <u>Indian</u>.

3. Something from **Austria** _____ is <u>Austrian</u>.

4. Something from **Egypt** _____ is <u>Egyptian</u>.

5. Something from **Korea** _____ is <u>Korean</u>.

▶Review

GRAMMAR AND USAGE

Rule

▶The word **I, proper nouns, titles,** and initials in a name are always capitalized.

▶**Conjunctions** connect words or groups of words.

▶**Interjections** show strong feeling or emotions.

Rule

▶A **comma** (,) separates the quotation marks from the rest of the sentence.

▶**Apostrophes** (') are used in contractions.

▶**Colons** (:) are used before a list of items in a series.

Practice

▶Rewrite the sentences with correct capitalization and punctuation.

1. dr. t.j. lopez is going to bring these items to the picnic bread, butter, and napkins. <u>Dr. T.J. Lopez is going to</u> <u>bring these items to the picnic: bread, butter, and napkins.</u>

_____

▶Underline the conjunctions in the sentences.

2. The park is on the corner of State Street <u>and</u> Main Street.

3. Should take the bus <u>or</u> the train?

WRITER'S CRAFT

► Supporting Details

> ►The **main idea** is what a paragraph is about.
>
> ►**Supporting details** tell about the main idea.

Practice   Write the details under the main ideas they match.

Main Ideas:

Spring is the best season
The flowers finally bloom. The weather gets warmer.

You can play baseball.

Computers are useful
You can write papers on them. They allow you to write to friends and family in other states.
You can look up information on them.

Details:

You can write papers on them.

The flowers finally bloom.

The weather gets warmer.

They allow you to write to friends and family in other states.

You can look up information on them.

You can play baseball.

▶Fact and Opinion

Focus A story can include both facts and opinions about things or people. Story characters can have opinions, too.

▶A **fact** can be checked and proven true.
  It *is a fact that lox is smoked salmon.*

▶An **opinion** cannot be proven. It is one person's idea.
  It *is an opinion when Pablo says that he does not like lox.*

Practice

▶Write whether the sentence gives a fact or an opinion.

1. __opinion__ Fruits are the best food.

2. __fact__ Tomatoes are usually red when ripe.

3. __fact__ There are many ways to cook potatoes.

4. __opinion__ Children should be taught to cook.

5. __opinion__ Ice cream is the best dessert.

6. __fact__ Bagels are made from dough.

7. __fact__ Bananas grow on trees.

8. __opinion__ Cream cheese tastes good on bagels.

COMPREHENSION

▶**Fact and Opinion**

COMPREHENSION

9. opinion _____ Apples taste better than bananas.

10. opinion _____ Meatloaf is the best dinner.

▶**Read the following paragraph. Draw a line under each sentence that tells a fact. Circle the sentences that give opinions.**

(Cooking is a lot of fun.) Some people are chefs. Their job is to cook. Many chefs go to cooking school. Both men and women can be chefs. (Home cooking is better than a chef's cooking.) Hotels, restaurants, schools, and even airlines have chefs. (It would be a fun job to be a chef.)

Apply Write a sentence that gives an opinion about your favorite cereal. **Answers will vary.**

_____

_____

_____

▶Review

| eight into notebook whatever peace |

Visualization Strategy
Circle the word that is spelled correctly.
Then write the word.

1. notbook   (notebook)   **notebook** _____

2. (whatever)   whatevir   **whatever** _____

3. peece   (peace)   **peace** _____

4. (eight)   aght   **eight** _____

5. innto   (into)   **into** _____

SPELLING

▶Review

A **suffix** is added to the end of a word. The suffix *-less* may change a word so that it means "without."

color + less = "without color"

The white rat was <u>colorless</u>.

VOCABULARY

▶Draw a line from the word with *-less* added to the words that tell what it means.

1. painless   without thought

2. harmless   without harm

3. thoughtless   without pain

▶Add the suffix *-less*, then write what the word means.

Answers may vary.

4. use + less = <u>**useless**</u>

    meaning: <u>**without use**</u>

5. hair + less = <u>**hairless**</u>

    meaning: <u>**without hair**</u>

Review

> **Rule**
>
> ▶ **Adjectives** describe or tell more about a noun or pronoun.
>
> ▶ **Adverbs** describe a verb.
>
> ▶ **Plural nouns** name more than one person, place, or thing.

GRAMMAR AND USAGE

Practice

▶ **Circle the correct plural for each singular noun.**

Singular	Plural	
1. peach	peachs	(peaches)
2. grape	(grapes)	grapies

▶ **Underline the adjective and circle the adverb.**

3. (Sadly) we said goodbye to our <u>new</u> neighbors.

4. We walked (slowly) to the <u>swimming</u> pool.

UNIT 6 Our Country and Its People • **Lesson 7** *Jalapeño Bagels*

WRITER'S CRAFT

▶Plagiarism

> **Plagiarism** is presenting someone else's ideas or words as your own. Always write papers in your own words.

Practice **Read the paragraph. Then rewrite it in your own words.**

Blue whales are the biggest animals in the world. They weigh 209 tons. They live near the north and south poles when it is warm. When it gets cold, they swim to a warmer place. They eat tiny sea creatures called krill. They eat four tons of food a day. That is a lot of krill!

Answers will vary.

_____

_____

_____

_____

_____

_____

_____

Plagiarism • Reteach